TABLE OF CONTENTS

All-Time Favorites

Vanilla Whoopie Pies with Chocolate-Hazelnut Cream

Cookies

2¼ cups all-purpose flour
2 teaspoons baking powder
½ teaspoon salt
1 cup packed brown sugar
½ cup (1 stick) butter, softened
2 eggs
¾ cup milk, at room temperature
2 teaspoons vanilla paste *or* seeds from 1 vanilla bean

Filling

½ cup (1 stick) butter, softened
4 ounces cream cheese, softened
½ cup chocolate-hazelnut spread
1 cup powdered sugar
1½ teaspoons vanilla

1. For cookies, preheat oven to 350°F. Line two cookie sheets with parchment paper. Sift flour, baking powder and salt into medium bowl.

2. Beat brown sugar and ½ cup butter in large bowl with electric mixer at medium speed 5 minutes or until light and fluffy. Add eggs, one at a time, beating well after each addition. Beat in flour mixture at low speed until combined. Add milk and vanilla paste; beat until blended. Drop rounded tablespoonfuls of batter 2 inches apart onto prepared cookie sheets.

3. Bake 10 to 12 minutes or until cookies spring back when lightly touched. Cool 2 minutes on cookie sheets. Remove to wire racks; cool completely.

4. For filling, beat ½ cup butter, cream cheese and chocolate-hazelnut spread in large bowl with electric mixer at medium speed until creamy. Add powdered sugar and vanilla; beat until smooth.

5. Pipe or spread 2 tablespoons filling on flat side of half of cookies; top with remaining cookies. *Makes 20 whoopie pies*

Mini Chocolate Whoopie Pies

Cookies

 1¾ cups all-purpose flour
 ½ cup unsweetened Dutch process cocoa powder
 ¾ teaspoon baking powder
 ½ teaspoon baking soda
 ½ teaspoon salt
 1 cup packed brown sugar
 ½ cup (1 stick) butter, softened
 1 egg
 1 teaspoon vanilla
 1 cup milk

Filling

 1 cup marshmallow creme
 1 cup powdered sugar
 ½ cup (1 stick) butter, softened
 ½ teaspoon vanilla

1. For cookies, preheat oven to 350°F. Line two cookie sheets with parchment paper. Sift flour, cocoa, baking powder, baking soda and salt into medium bowl.

2. Beat brown sugar and ½ cup butter in large bowl with electric mixer at medium-high speed about 3 minutes or until light and fluffy. Beat in egg and 1 teaspoon vanilla until well blended. Alternately add flour mixture and milk, beating at low speed after each addition until smooth and well blended. Drop dough by heaping teaspoonfuls 2 inches apart onto prepared cookie sheets.

3. Bake 8 to 10 minutes or until cookies are puffed and tops spring back when lightly touched. Cool 10 minutes on cookie sheets. Remove to wire racks; cool completely.

4. For filling, beat marshmallow creme, powdered sugar, ½ cup butter and ½ teaspoon vanilla in large bowl with electric mixer at high speed 2 minutes or until light and fluffy.

5. Pipe or spread heaping teaspoon filling on flat side of half of cookies; top with remaining cookies.   *Makes about 24 mini whoopie pies*

Peanut Butter & Jelly Whoopie Pies

Cookies
> 1 package (about 18 ounces) white cake mix, plus ingredients to prepare mix

Filling
> 1½ cups powdered sugar
> ⅔ cup peanut butter
> ¼ cup whipping cream
> 1 tablespoon butter, softened
> ½ cup jam, any flavor

1. For cookies, preheat oven to 350°F. Spray two whoopie pie pans with nonstick cooking spray.

2. Prepare cake mix according to package directions. Spoon 2 tablespoons batter into each prepared whoopie pie cup.

3. Bake 10 to 11 minutes or until cookies spring back when lightly touched. Cool 2 minutes in pans. Remove to wire racks; cool completely.

4. For filling, beat powdered sugar, peanut butter, cream and butter in large bowl with electric mixer at medium speed until light and fluffy.

5. Spread 2 tablespoons filling on flat sides of half of cookies; spread 1 tablespoon jam on flat sides of remaining cookies. Make sandwiches.

Makes 16 whoopie pies

 TIP When using whoopie pie pans, be sure to let them cool completely before adding more batter. Wipe them with a paper towel and spray again with nonstick cooking spray.

Lemon Lovers' Whoopie Pies

Cookies
- 1½ cups all-purpose flour
- ½ teaspoon baking powder
- ¼ teaspoon baking soda
- ¼ teaspoon salt
- 1¼ cups granulated sugar
- 6 tablespoons (¾ stick) butter, softened
- 2 teaspoons grated lemon peel
- 2 eggs
- 2 tablespoons lemon juice
- 1½ teaspoons vanilla
- ½ cup buttermilk

Filling
- 1 package (8 ounces) cream cheese, softened
- 6 tablespoons (¾ stick) butter, softened
- 1 teaspoon vanilla
- 2 tablespoons lemon juice
- 2 teaspoons grated lemon peel
- 3 cups powdered sugar

1. For cookies, preheat oven to 350°F. Line two cookie sheets with parchment paper. Combine flour, baking powder, baking soda and salt in medium bowl.

2. Beat granulated sugar, 6 tablespoons butter and 2 teaspoons lemon peel in large bowl with electric mixer at medium speed about 2 minutes or until creamy. Add eggs, 2 tablespoons lemon juice and 1½ teaspoons vanilla; beat about 1 minute or until well blended.

3. Add half of flour mixture; beat at low speed just until blended. Add buttermilk and remaining flour mixture; beat just until blended. Drop 3 tablespoonfuls of batter 3 inches apart onto prepared cookie sheets.

4. Bake 12 to 13 minutes until edges are lightly browned. Cool 10 minutes on cookie sheets. Remove to wire racks; cool completely.

5. For filling, beat cream cheese, 6 tablespoons butter, 1 teaspoon vanilla, 2 tablespoons lemon juice and 2 teaspoons lemon peel in medium bowl with electric mixer at medium speed about 1 minute or until well blended. Add powdered sugar; beat 3 minutes or until light and fluffy.

6. Pipe or spread 3 tablespoons filling on flat side of half of cookies; top with remaining cookies.   *Makes 13 whoopie pies*

S'More Whoopie Pies

Cookies
- 1½ cups graham cracker crumbs (8 whole graham crackers)
- 1¼ cups all-purpose flour
- 1½ teaspoons baking powder
- ½ teaspoon salt
- ½ cup (1 stick) butter, softened
- ½ cup granulated sugar
- ½ cup packed brown sugar
- 1 egg
- ½ cup buttermilk
- 1 teaspoon baking soda
- 1 teaspoon white vinegar
- ¼ teaspoon ground cinnamon
- 1 teaspoon vanilla

Ganache
- ¾ cup whipping cream
- 1 tablespoon butter
- 1 package (12 ounces) semisweet chocolate chips
- 1 tablespoon vanilla

Filling
- 1½ cups marshmallow creme
- 1¼ cups shortening
- 1 cup powdered sugar
- 1 tablespoon vanilla

1. For cookies, preheat oven to 350°F. Line two cookie sheets with parchment paper. Combine crumbs, flour, baking powder and salt in medium bowl.

2. Beat ½ cup butter, granulated sugar and brown sugar in large bowl with electric mixer at medium speed about 3 minutes or until light and fluffy. Add egg; beat until well blended.

3. Whisk buttermilk, baking soda, vinegar and cinnamon in small bowl. Add to butter mixture; beat at low speed just until blended. Add 1 teaspoon vanilla; beat at medium speed 2 minutes or until well blended. Add flour mixture; beat just until blended. Drop rounded 1½ tablespoonfuls of batter 2 inches apart onto prepared cookie sheets.

4. Bake 10 to 12 minutes until cookies just begin to brown. Cool 10 minutes on cookie sheets. Remove to wire racks; cool completely.

5. For ganache, combine cream and 1 tablespoon butter in small saucepan; bring to a simmer over medium heat. Remove from heat; stir in chocolate chips and vanilla until chocolate is melted and mixture is smooth. Let stand about 15 minutes or until thickened.

6. For filling, beat marshmallow creme and shortening in medium bowl with electric mixer at low speed until smooth. Beat at medium speed about 3 minutes or until fluffy. Add powdered sugar and 1 tablespoon vanilla; beat at medium speed 3 minutes or until light and fluffy.

7. Pipe or spread 2 tablespoons marshmallow filling on flat side of half of cookies. Spread about 1 tablespoon ganache over filling; top with remaining cookies.   *Makes 20 whoopie pies*

Carrot Cake Whoopie Pies

Cookies

2 cups all-purpose flour
1½ teaspoons baking soda
1¼ teaspoons ground cinnamon
1 teaspoon baking powder
1 teaspoon ground ginger
½ teaspoon salt
½ teaspoon ground nutmeg
⅛ teaspoon ground cloves
½ cup (1 stick) butter, softened
½ cup granulated sugar
½ cup packed brown sugar
2 eggs
1½ teaspoons vanilla
1½ cups grated carrots (4 to 5 carrots)

Filling

1 package (8 ounces) cream cheese, softened
½ cup (1 stick) butter, softened
¾ cup powdered sugar
½ cup packed brown sugar
½ teaspoon vanilla
¼ teaspoon ground cinnamon
¼ teaspoon ground nutmeg
⅛ teaspoon ground allspice

1. For cookies, sift flour, baking soda, 1¼ teaspoons cinnamon, baking powder, ginger, salt, ½ teaspoon nutmeg and cloves into medium bowl.

2. Beat ½ cup butter, granulated sugar and ½ cup brown sugar in large bowl with electric mixer at medium speed 5 minutes or until light and fluffy. Add eggs, one at a time, beating well after each addition. Beat in 1½ teaspoons vanilla. Beat in flour mixture at low speed just until combined. Stir in carrots. Cover and refrigerate 1 hour.

3. Preheat oven to 350°F. Line two cookie sheets with parchment paper. Drop rounded tablespoonfuls of batter 2 inches apart onto prepared cookie sheets.

4. Bake 10 to 12 minutes or until cookies spring back when lightly touched. Cool 2 minutes on cookie sheets. Remove to wire racks; cool completely.

5. For filling, beat cream cheese and ½ cup butter in large bowl with electric mixer at medium speed until light and fluffy. Beat in powdered sugar, ½ cup brown sugar, ½ teaspoon vanilla, ¼ teaspoon cinnamon, ¼ teaspoon nutmeg and allspice until smooth.

6. Pipe or spread 2 tablespoons filling on flat side of half of cookies; top with remaining cookies.   *Makes 16 whoopie pies*

Boston Cream Whoopie Pies

Filling
1½ cups half-and-half
½ cup sugar
2 eggs
1 egg yolk
2½ tablespoons all-purpose flour
1 teaspoon vanilla

Cookies
2¼ cups all-purpose flour
1½ teaspoons baking powder
¼ teaspoon salt
1 cup sugar
6 tablespoons (¾ stick) butter, softened
2 eggs
⅔ cup buttermilk
2 teaspoons vanilla

Ganache
¼ cup whipping cream
1 tablespoon butter
1 cup chocolate chips
½ teaspoon vanilla

1. For filling, bring half-and-half to a simmer in medium heavy saucepan over medium heat. Whisk ½ cup sugar, 2 eggs, egg yolk and 2½ tablespoons flour in medium bowl until well blended. Gradually whisk in hot half-and-half. Pour mixture back into saucepan over medium heat, whisking until mixture thickens and comes to a boil. Boil 1 minute, whisking constantly. Pour into medium bowl; stir in 1 teaspoon vanilla. Cover and refrigerate at least 4 hours.

2. For cookies, preheat oven to 350°F. Line two cookie sheets with parchment paper. Combine 2¼ cups flour, baking powder and salt in medium bowl.

3. Beat 1 cup sugar and 6 tablespoons butter in large bowl with electric mixer at medium-high speed 3 minutes or until light and fluffy. Add eggs; beat 1 minute or until well blended. Beat in half of flour mixture until blended; beat in buttermilk and 2 teaspoons vanilla. Add remaining flour mixture; beat just until blended. Drop 2 rounded tablespoonfuls of batter 2 inches apart onto prepared cookie sheets.

4. Bake 13 to 15 minutes or until edges are lightly browned. Cool 5 minutes on cookie sheets. Remove to wire racks; cool completely.

5. For ganache, combine cream and 1 tablespoon butter in small saucepan; bring to a simmer over medium heat. Remove from heat; stir in chocolate chips and ½ teaspoon vanilla until chocolate is melted and mixture is smooth. Keep warm.

6. Spread 1 tablespoon ganache over tops of half of cookies; let stand about 10 minutes or until set. Pipe or spread 2 tablespoons filling on flat side of remaining cookies; top with ganache-covered cookies. Garnish with cherries.

Makes 16 whoopie pies

Chocolate Chip Oatmeal Cream Pies

Cookies
1½ cups old-fashioned oats
1½ cups all-purpose flour
2 teaspoons baking powder
½ teaspoon salt
½ teaspoon ground cinnamon
1 cup packed brown sugar
½ cup (1 stick) butter, softened
1 egg
½ cup milk
½ cup mini semisweet chocolate chips, divided

Filling
1 jar (7 ounces) marshmallow creme
1½ cups powdered sugar
½ cup (1 stick) butter, softened

1. For cookies, preheat oven to 350°F. Line two cookie sheets with parchment paper. Combine oats, flour, baking powder, salt and cinnamon in medium bowl.

2. Beat brown sugar and ½ cup butter in large bowl with electric mixer at medium speed until blended. Beat in egg until well blended. Add oat mixture, milk and ¼ cup chocolate chips; beat at low speed just until combined.

3. Drop teaspoonfuls of batter 2 inches apart onto prepared cookie sheets. Sprinkle with remaining ¼ cup chocolate chips.

4. Bake about 13 minutes or until edges are light golden brown. Remove to wire racks; cool completely.

5. For filling, beat marshmallow creme, powdered sugar and ½ cup butter in large bowl with electric mixer at medium-high speed until well blended and fluffy.

6. Pipe or spread filling on flat side of half of cookies; top with remaining cookies. *Makes about 36 whoopie pies*

Peanut Butter Fudge Whoopies

Cookies
- 1½ cups plus 2 tablespoons all-purpose flour
- 1 teaspoon baking powder
- 1 teaspoon baking soda
- ½ cup granulated sugar
- ½ cup packed brown sugar
- ½ cup creamy peanut butter
- ¼ cup (½ stick) butter, softened
- 1 egg
- 1 teaspoon vanilla
- ½ cup milk

Filling
- 16 ounces semisweet chocolate, chopped
- ½ cup creamy peanut butter
- 1½ cups whipping cream
- ½ cup chopped peanuts

1. For cookies, combine flour, baking powder and baking soda in medium bowl.

2. Beat granulated sugar, brown sugar, ½ cup peanut butter and butter in large bowl with electric mixer at medium-high speed until creamy. Add egg and vanilla; beat at medium speed 2 minutes. Add flour mixture and milk; beat at low speed just until combined. Cover and refrigerate 30 minutes.

3. Preheat oven to 350°F. Line two cookie sheets with parchment paper. Drop tablespoonfuls of batter 2 inches apart onto prepared cookie sheets.

4. Bake 14 minutes or until light brown around edges. Cool 5 minutes on cookie sheets. Remove to wire racks; cool completely.

5. For filling, place chocolate and ½ cup peanut butter in large bowl. Heat cream to a simmer in small saucepan over low heat. Pour over chocolate and peanut butter. Let stand 2 minutes; stir until well blended. Refrigerate 30 minutes or until firm. Beat with electric mixer at medium-high speed until thick and creamy.

6. Pipe or spread filling on flat side of half of cookies; top with remaining cookies. Place peanuts in shallow dish; roll edges of cookies in peanuts.

Makes 14 whoopie pies

Red Velvet Whoopies

Cookies

1¾ cups all-purpose flour
½ teaspoon baking powder
½ teaspoon baking soda
¼ teaspoon salt
2 tablespoons red food coloring
1½ tablespoons unsweetened cocoa powder
½ cup (1 stick) butter, softened
½ cup granulated sugar
½ cup packed brown sugar
1 egg
1 teaspoon vanilla
⅓ cup buttermilk
2 teaspoons apple cider vinegar

Filling

1 package (8 ounces) cream cheese, softened
½ cup (1 stick) butter, softened
1 teaspoon vanilla
2½ cups powdered sugar

1. For cookies, preheat oven to 350°F. Line two cookie sheets with parchment paper. Combine flour, baking powder, baking soda and salt in medium bowl.

2. Combine food coloring and cocoa in large bowl; whisk until smooth paste is formed. Add ½ cup butter, granulated sugar and brown sugar; beat with electric mixer at medium speed 3 minutes or until smooth and fluffy. Add egg and 1 teaspoon vanilla; beat 1 minute. Add buttermilk and vinegar; beat 1 minute. Add flour mixture; beat at low speed just until combined. Drop tablespoonfuls of batter onto prepared cookie sheets.

3. Bake 10 minutes or until tops spring back when lightly touched. Cool 5 minutes on cookie sheets. Remove to wire racks; cool completely.

4. For filling, beat cream cheese, ½ cup butter and 1 teaspoon vanilla with electric mixer at medium speed until creamy. Add powdered sugar; beat until creamy and spreadable.

5. Pipe or spread filling on flat side of half of cookies; top with remaining cookies.   *Makes about 18 whoopie pies*

Supersize Whoopie Pies

Cookies
- 2 cups all-purpose flour
- 1½ teaspoons baking soda
- 1 teaspoon salt
- ¾ cup packed brown sugar
- ½ cup (1 stick) butter, softened
- ¼ cup granulated sugar
- 1 egg
- 1 teaspoon vanilla
- 1 cup buttermilk

Filling
- ¾ cup powdered sugar
- ½ cup (1 stick) butter, softened
- 1 jar (7 ounces) marshmallow creme
- 1 teaspoon vanilla

1. For cookies, preheat oven to 350°F. Line two cookie sheets with parchment paper. Combine flour, baking soda and salt in small bowl.

2. Beat brown sugar, ½ cup butter and granulated sugar in large bowl with electric mixer until creamy. Add egg and 1 teaspoon vanilla; beat until well blended. Alternately add flour mixture and buttermilk, beating until blended after each addition. Drop scant ¼ cupfuls of batter 2 to 3 inches apart onto prepared cookie sheets.

3. Bake 10 to 12 minutes or until set. Cool 5 minutes on cookie sheets. Remove to wire racks; cool completely.

4. For filling, beat powdered sugar and ½ cup butter in large bowl with electric mixer at medium speed until light and fluffy. Add marshmallow creme and 1 teaspoon vanilla; beat until smooth.

5. Spread 3 tablespoons filling on flat side of half of cookies; top with remaining cookies. *Makes 8 whoopie pies*

Pistachio Whoopie Pies

Cookies
- 1½ cups all-purpose flour
- ¾ teaspoon baking powder
- ½ teaspoon ground cardamom
- ½ teaspoon salt
- ¾ cup packed brown sugar
- ¼ cup (½ stick) butter, softened
- 1 egg
- ½ teaspoon vanilla
- ⅓ cup buttermilk
- ¼ cup plus 3 tablespoons finely chopped pistachio nuts, divided

Filling
- 2 cups powdered sugar
- 5 tablespoons butter, softened
- 3 tablespoons whipping cream
- 1 teaspoon vanilla

1. For cookies, preheat oven to 350°F. Line two cookie sheets with parchment paper. Combine flour, baking powder, cardamom and ½ teaspoon salt in medium bowl.

2. Beat brown sugar and ¼ cup butter in large bowl with electric mixer at medium speed 1 minute or until blended. Add egg and ½ teaspoon vanilla; beat 1 minute or until well blended. Add half of flour mixture and half of buttermilk; beat at low speed just until combined. Add remaining flour mixture and buttermilk; beat about 2 minutes or until well blended. Stir in ¼ cup pistachios. Drop 2 tablespoonfuls of batter 2 inches apart onto prepared cookie sheets; sprinkle with remaining 3 tablespoons pistachios.

3. Bake 11 to 13 minutes or until golden brown around edges. Cool 5 minutes on cookie sheets. Remove to wire racks; cool completely.

4. For filling, beat powdered sugar and 5 tablespoons butter in large bowl with electric mixer at medium speed 1 minute or until crumbly. Add cream and 1 teaspoon vanilla; beat at high speed 2 minutes or until creamy.

5. Pipe or spread 2 tablespoons filling on flat side of half of cookies; top with remaining cookies.   *Makes 22 whoopie pies*

Pumpkin Whoopie Minis

Cookies

1¾ cups all-purpose flour
2 teaspoons pumpkin pie spice
1 teaspoon baking powder
1 teaspoon baking soda
¾ teaspoon salt
1 cup packed brown sugar
¼ cup (½ stick) butter, softened
1 cup canned solid-pack pumpkin
2 eggs, lightly beaten
¼ cup vegetable oil
½ teaspoon vanilla

Filling

4 ounces cream cheese, softened
¼ cup (½ stick) butter, softened
½ teaspoon vanilla
¼ teaspoon salt
1½ cups powdered sugar

1. For cookies, preheat oven to 350°F. Line two cookie sheets with parchment paper. Combine flour, pumpkin pie spice, baking powder, baking soda and ¾ teaspoon salt in medium bowl.

2. Beat brown sugar and ¼ cup butter in large bowl with electric mixer at medium speed until creamy. Beat in pumpkin, eggs, oil and ½ teaspoon vanilla until well blended. Beat in flour mixture at low speed just until blended. Drop teaspoonfuls of batter 2 inches apart onto prepared cookie sheets.

3. Bake 10 to 12 minutes or until tops spring back when lightly touched. Cool 5 minutes on cookie sheets. Remove to wire racks; cool completely.

4. For filling, beat cream cheese and ¼ cup butter in medium bowl with electric mixer until smooth and creamy. Beat in ½ teaspoon vanilla and ¼ teaspoon salt until blended. Gradually add powdered sugar; beat until light and fluffy.

5. Pipe or spread heaping teaspoon filling on flat side of half of cookies; top with remaining cookies.   *Makes about 30 mini whoopie pies*

Tiramisu Whoopie Pies

Cookies
- 2 cups all-purpose flour
- 1½ teaspoons baking soda
- ½ teaspoon salt
- 1 cup granulated sugar
- ¾ cup (1½ sticks) butter, softened
- 1 egg
- ¼ cup milk

Filling
- 8 ounces mascarpone cheese
- 1½ tablespoons packed brown sugar
- 1½ tablespoons vanilla
- ¾ teaspoon instant espresso powder dissolved in 1½ teaspoons hot water
- Unsweetened cocoa powder (optional)

1. For cookies, preheat oven to 350°F. Line two cookie sheets with parchment paper. Sift flour, baking soda and salt into medium bowl.

2. Beat granulated sugar and butter in large bowl with electric mixer at medium speed 5 minutes or until light and fluffy. Beat in egg until blended. Add half of flour mixture and milk; beat just until combined. Beat in remaining flour mixture until smooth. Drop rounded tablespoonfuls of batter 2 inches apart onto prepared cookie sheets.

3. Bake 10 to 12 minutes or until lightly browned around edges. Cool 2 minutes on cookie sheets. Remove to wire racks; cool completely.

4. For filling, beat mascarpone and brown sugar in large bowl with electric mixer at medium speed until well blended. Add vanilla and espresso mixture; beat until smooth.

5. Spread 2 tablespoons filling on flat side of half of cookies; top with remaining cookies. Dust edges of cookies with cocoa, if desired.

Makes 20 whoopie pies

Fabulous Fruit

Banana-Peanut Butter Whoopie Pies

Cookies
- 1¼ cups all-purpose flour
- ½ teaspoon baking soda
- ½ teaspoon baking powder
- ½ teaspoon salt
- ½ cup packed brown sugar
- ½ cup vegetable oil
- 1 large banana, mashed
- ½ cup sour cream
- 1 egg
- 1 teaspoon vanilla

Filling
- 4 ounces cream cheese, softened
- 1½ cups creamy peanut butter
- 2 tablespoons butter, softened
- 2 tablespoons milk
- 2 cups powdered sugar

1. For cookies, preheat oven to 350°F. Line two cookie sheets with parchment paper. Combine flour, baking soda, baking powder and salt in medium bowl.

2. Beat brown sugar, oil, banana and sour cream in large bowl with electric mixer at medium speed until creamy. Add egg and vanilla; beat 2 minutes. Add flour mixture; beat at low speed just until combined. Spoon tablespoonfuls of batter 2 inches apart onto prepared cookie sheets.

3. Bake 10 minutes or until lightly browned around edges. Cool 2 minutes on cookie sheets. Remove to wire racks; cool completely.

4. For filling, beat cream cheese in large bowl with electric mixer at medium-high speed until creamy. Add peanut butter, butter and milk; beat until smooth. Add powdered sugar; beat at medium speed until creamy and spreadable.

5. Pipe or spread filling on flat side of half of cookies; top with remaining cookies. *Makes 12 whoopie pies*

Strawberry Whoopie Pies

Cookies

- 3½ cups all-purpose flour
- 1½ teaspoons baking powder
- 1 teaspoon baking soda
- ½ teaspoon salt
- 1 cup stemmed and halved strawberries
- 2 cups packed brown sugar
- ½ cup vegetable oil
- ½ cup plain yogurt
- 2 teaspoons vanilla
- 3 eggs

Filling

- 1 package (4-serving size) instant vanilla pudding and pie filling mix
- ½ cup milk
- 1 teaspoon vanilla
- 1 container (8 ounces) frozen whipped topping, thawed
- 1½ cups chopped fresh strawberries
  Powdered sugar (optional)

1. For cookies, sift flour, baking powder, baking soda and salt into medium bowl. Place halved strawberries in food processor; process with on/off pulses until very finely chopped.

2. Whisk brown sugar and oil in large bowl until well blended. Whisk in chopped strawberries, yogurt and 2 teaspoons vanilla. Whisk in eggs just until combined. Fold in flour mixture just until blended. Cover and refrigerate 30 minutes.

3. Preheat oven 350°F. Line two cookie sheets with parchment paper. Drop rounded tablespoonfuls of batter 2 inches apart onto prepared cookie sheets.

4. Bake 12 to 15 minutes or until cookies spring back when lightly touched. Cool 2 minutes on cookie sheets. Remove to wire racks; cool completely.

5. For filling, whisk pudding mix, milk and 1 teaspoon vanilla in large bowl until smooth. Fold in whipped topping until blended.

6. Spread filling on flat sides of cookies; top half with chopped strawberries, filling and remaining cookies. Sprinkle with powdered sugar, if desired.

Makes 10 whoopie pies

Grapefruit Whoopie Pies

Cookies

3 cups sifted cake flour
2½ teaspoons baking powder
½ teaspoon salt
1¾ cups granulated sugar
1 cup (2 sticks) butter, softened
2 eggs
½ cup grapefruit juice
¾ cup milk
1½ teaspoons vanilla
1 teaspoon grated grapefruit peel

Filling

½ cup shortening
½ cup (1 stick) butter, softened
3 tablespoons grapefruit juice
1½ teaspoons grated grapefruit peel
4 cups powdered sugar

1. For cookies, preheat oven to 350°F. Spray two whoopie pie pans with nonstick cooking spray; dust lightly with flour. Combine flour, baking powder and salt in medium bowl.

2. Beat granulated sugar and 1 cup butter in large bowl with electric mixer at medium speed 5 minutes or until light and fluffy. Add eggs, one at a time, beating well after each addition. Add flour mixture alternately with ½ cup grapefruit juice, beginning and ending with flour mixture. Gradually beat in milk. Stir in 1½ teaspoons vanilla and 1 teaspoon grapefruit peel; mix well. Spoon 2 tablespoons of batter into each prepared whoopie pie cup.

3. Bake 12 to 15 minutes or until cookies spring back when lightly touched. Cool 2 minutes in pans. Remove to wire racks; cool completely. (Pans should be completely cooled, washed, sprayed and dusted with flour in between batches.)

4. For filling, beat shortening and ½ cup butter in large bowl with electric mixer at medium-high speed about 4 minutes or until light and fluffy. Add 3 tablespoons grapefruit juice and 1½ teaspoons grapefruit peel; beat until blended. Gradually add powdered sugar, beating until well blended.

5. Pipe or spread 2 tablespoons filling on flat side of half of cookies; top with remaining cookies.   *Makes 24 whoopie pies*

Lemon Raspberry Whoopie Pies

Cookies

2¼ cups all-purpose flour
¾ teaspoon baking powder
½ teaspoon salt
¼ teaspoon baking soda
1 cup packed brown sugar
½ cup (1 stick) butter, softened
1 egg
2 tablespoons grated lemon peel
2 tablespoons whipping cream
1½ teaspoons vanilla
1 teaspoon lemon juice
1 cup vanilla yogurt

Filling

1 cup whipping cream
¼ cup powdered sugar, plus additional for garnish
1¼ cups fresh or thawed frozen raspberries
1 tablespoon grated lemon peel

1. For cookies, preheat oven to 350°F. Line two cookie sheets with parchment paper. Sift flour, baking powder, salt and baking soda into medium bowl.

2. Beat brown sugar and butter in large bowl with electric mixer at medium speed 5 minutes or until light and fluffy. Beat in egg, 2 tablespoons lemon peel, 2 tablespoons cream, vanilla and lemon juice. Add half of flour mixture and ½ cup yogurt; beat until blended. Beat in remaining flour mixture and yogurt until smooth. Drop rounded tablespoonfuls of batter 2 inches apart onto prepared cookie sheets.

3. Bake 10 to 12 minutes or until cookies spring back when lightly touched. Cool 2 minutes on cookie sheets. Remove to wire racks; cool completely.

4. For filling, beat 1 cup cream and ¼ cup powdered sugar in large bowl with electric mixer at medium-high speed until stiff peaks form. Mash raspberries and 1 tablespoon lemon peel with fork in small bowl; fold into whipped cream.

5. Spread 2 tablespoons filling on flat side of half of cookies; top with remaining cookies. Sprinkle with additional powdered sugar.

Makes 20 whoopie pies

Applesauce Spice Whoopie Pies

Cookies

>   3 cups plus 1 tablespoon all-purpose flour, divided
>   2 teaspoons baking soda
>   1 teaspoon ground cinnamon
>   ½ teaspoon ground nutmeg
>   ¼ teaspoon salt
>   1 cup raisins
> 1½ cups packed dark brown sugar
>   ½ cup (1 stick) butter, softened
>   1 cup chunky applesauce
>   ¼ cup apple butter
>   2 egg whites
>   1 egg
>   ½ cup finely chopped peeled Golden Delicious or other sweet apple

Filling

>   4 ounces cream cheese, softened
>   ¼ cup (½ stick) butter, softened
>   2 cups sifted powdered sugar
>   ¼ cup apple butter
>   ¾ teaspoon ground cinnamon
>   ¼ teaspoon ground nutmeg
>   1 tablespoon apple juice
>   ½ teaspoon vanilla

1. For cookies, preheat oven to 350°F. Spray two whoopie pie pans with nonstick cooking spray. Sift 3 cups flour, baking soda, 1 teaspoon cinnamon, ½ teaspoon nutmeg and salt into medium bowl. Place raisins in small bowl; cover with hot water.

2. Beat brown sugar and ½ cup butter in large bowl with electric mixer at medium speed about 5 minutes or until light and fluffy. Add applesauce, ¼ cup apple butter, egg whites and egg; beat until blended. Add flour mixture; beat just until blended.

3. Drain raisins; pat dry and toss with remaining 1 tablespoon flour. Stir raisins and apple into batter. Spoon 2 tablespoons of batter into each prepared whoopie pie cup.

4. Bake 12 minutes or until toothpick inserted into centers comes out clean. Remove to wire racks; cool completely. (Pans should be completely cooled, washed and sprayed with cooking spray in between batches.)

5. For filling, beat cream cheese and ¼ cup butter in large bowl with electric mixer at high speed about 3 minutes or until light and fluffy. Add powdered sugar, ¼ cup apple butter, ¾ teaspoon cinnamon and ¼ teaspoon nutmeg; beat at medium-low speed until well blended. Add apple juice and vanilla, beat 1 minute or until blended.

6. Spread scant 2 tablespoons filling on flat side of half of cookies; top with remaining cookies.   *Makes 18 whoopie pies*

Banana-Hazelnut Whoopie Pies

Cookies
- 2 cups all-purpose flour
- 1 teaspoon salt
- 1 teaspoon ground cinnamon
- ½ teaspoon baking soda
- ½ teaspoon baking powder
- ½ cup (1 stick) butter, softened
- ½ cup granulated sugar
- ½ cup packed dark brown sugar
- 1 egg
- 1½ teaspoons vanilla
- 1 cup mashed ripe bananas (about 2 medium bananas)
- ½ cup sour cream

Filling
- ⅔ cup chocolate-hazelnut spread
- ½ cup (1 stick) butter, softened
- 1 cup powdered sugar
- 1½ tablespoons whipping cream
- 1 teaspoon vanilla

1. For cookies, preheat oven to 350°F. Line two cookie sheets with parchment paper. Sift flour, salt, cinnamon, baking soda and baking powder into medium bowl.

2. Beat ½ cup butter, granulated sugar and brown sugar in large bowl with electric mixer at medium speed 5 minutes or until light and fluffy. Beat in egg and 1½ teaspoons vanilla. Add bananas and sour cream; beat at low speed until blended. Beat in flour mixture until combined. Drop rounded tablespoonfuls of batter 2 inches apart onto prepared cookie sheets.

3. Bake 10 to 12 minutes or until cookies spring back when lightly touched. Cool 2 minutes on cookie sheets. Remove to wire racks; cool completely.

4. For filling, beat chocolate-hazelnut spread and ½ cup butter in large bowl with electric mixer at medium speed until smooth. Add powdered sugar, cream and 1 teaspoon vanilla; beat until smooth.

5. Pipe or spread 2 tablespoons filling on flat side of half of cookies; top with remaining cookies.   *Makes 20 whoopie pies*

Piña Colada Whoopie Pies

Cookies

    2 cups all-purpose flour
    1 teaspoon baking powder
    ¾ teaspoon baking soda
    ¼ teaspoon salt
    ½ cup (1 stick) butter, softened
    ¼ cup packed brown sugar
    2 eggs
    2 teaspoons rum extract
    ¼ cup cream of coconut
    1 can (about 8 ounces) crushed pineapple, undrained
    1½ cups sweetened flaked coconut

Filling

    3½ cups powdered sugar
    1 package (8 ounces) cream cheese, softened
    2 teaspoons rum extract
    ¼ cup sweetened flaked coconut

1. For cookies, preheat oven to 350°F. Line two cookie sheets with parchment paper. Combine flour, baking powder, baking soda and salt in medium bowl.

2. Beat butter and brown sugar in large bowl with electric mixer at medium speed about 2 minutes or until creamy. Add eggs and 2 teaspoons rum extract; beat 1 minute or until well blended.

3. Add half of flour mixture; beat just until blended. Beat in cream of coconut. Add remaining flour mixture and pineapple; beat 2 minutes or until well blended. Fold in 1½ cups coconut. Drop 2 level tablespoonfuls of batter 2 inches apart onto prepared cookie sheets.

4. Bake 11 to 13 minutes or until tops spring back when lightly touched. Cool 10 minutes on cookie sheets. Remove to wire racks; cool completely.

5. For filling, beat powdered sugar and cream cheese in large bowl with electric mixer at medium speed about 2 minutes or until light and fluffy. Add 2 teaspoons rum extract; beat 1 minute.

6. Pipe or spread 2 rounded tablespoons filling on flat side of half of cookies; top with remaining cookies. Place ¼ cup coconut in shallow dish; roll edges of cookies in coconut to coat lightly.   *Makes 20 whoopie pies*

Buttermilk Whoopie Pies with Lime Mousse Filling

Filling

- 1 teaspoon instant tapioca
- 2 tablespoons cold water
- 6 tablespoons fresh lime juice (about 3 limes)
- ½ cup sugar, divided
- 1 cup plain Greek yogurt
- 1 cup whipping cream

Cookies

- 2 cups all-purpose flour
- 1 teaspoon baking powder
- ¾ teaspoon baking soda
- ½ teaspoon salt
- 1⅓ cups sugar
- ½ cup (1 stick) butter, softened
- 2 eggs
- 1 teaspoon vanilla
- 1 cup buttermilk
- Grated lime peel (optional)

1. For filling, process tapioca in small food processor or coffee grinder 1 minute or until powdery. Stir into water in medium bowl; let stand 5 minutes. Combine lime juice and 6 tablespoons sugar in small saucepan; cook and stir over medium heat 3 minutes or until sugar is dissolved. Stir into tapioca mixture; let cool slightly. Whisk in yogurt.

2. Beat cream and remaining 2 tablespoons sugar in large bowl with electric mixer at medium-high speed until soft peaks form. Fold in lime mixture; refrigerate at least 1 hour or until set.

3. For cookies, preheat oven to 350°F. Line two cookie sheets with parchment paper. Sift flour, baking powder, baking soda and salt into medium bowl.

4. Beat 1⅓ cups sugar and butter in large bowl with electric mixer at medium speed 5 minutes or until light and fluffy. Add eggs, one at a time, beating well after each addition. Beat in vanilla. Alternately beat in flour mixture and buttermilk at low speed, beginning and ending with flour mixture. Drop rounded tablespoonfuls of batter 2 inches apart onto prepared cookie sheets.

5. Bake 10 minutes or until cookies spring back when lightly touched. Cool 2 minutes on cookie sheets. Remove to wire racks; cool completely.

6. Pipe or spread 2 tablespoons filling on flat side of half of cookies; top with remaining cookies. Sprinkle with lime peel, if desired.

Makes 22 whoopie pies

Orange Cornmeal Whoopie Pies

Filling
- ½ cup (1 stick) butter, softened
- 6 ounces cream cheese, softened
- 2 cups powdered sugar, sifted
- ½ cup orange marmalade
- 2 teaspoons orange juice
- 2 teaspoons grated orange peel

Cookies
- 1¼ cups granulated sugar, divided
- ½ cup plus 1 tablespoon olive oil, divided
- 2 eggs
- ¼ cup dry white wine
- ¼ cup orange juice
- 1¼ cups all-purpose flour
- ½ cup yellow cornmeal
- 2 tablespoons grated orange peel
- 2 teaspoons baking powder
- 1 teaspoon salt

1. For filling, beat butter and cream cheese in large bowl with electric mixer at medium-high speed 3 minutes or until light and fluffy. Add powdered sugar, 1 cup at a time, beating well after each addition. Add marmalade, 2 teaspoons orange juice and 2 teaspoons orange peel; beat 2 to 3 minutes or until well blended. Cover and refrigerate at least 1 hour.

2. For cookies, preheat oven to 375°F. Brush two whoopie pie pans with 1 tablespoon oil. Cut small rounds of parchment paper to fit bottoms of cups in whoopie pie pans. Line cups with parchment rounds; brush parchment with oil.

3. Whisk 1 cup granulated sugar, ½ cup oil, eggs, wine and ¼ cup orange juice in large bowl until smooth. Add flour, cornmeal, 2 tablespoons orange peel, baking powder and salt; whisk until well blended. Spoon 2 tablespoons batter into each prepared whoopie pie cup; sprinkle with remaining ¼ cup granulated sugar.

4. Bake 12 to 15 minutes or until toothpick inserted into centers comes out clean, rotating pans halfway through baking time. Cool 10 minutes in pans. Run knife around edge of each cookie to release; carefully remove from pans and peel off parchment paper. Cool completely on wire racks.

5. Spread 3 tablespoons filling on flat side of half of cookies; top with remaining cookies.   *Makes 12 whoopie pies*

Raspberry-Cream Whoopie Pie

Cookies

  1 cup all-purpose flour
  1 teaspoon baking powder
  ⅓ cup milk
  2 tablespoons butter
  ½ teaspoon vanilla
  6 eggs
  1 cup granulated sugar

Filling

  1 cup whipping cream
  ¼ cup powdered sugar
  ¼ teaspoon vanilla
  ¾ cup raspberry jelly or jam

1. For cookies, preheat oven to 350°F. Spray two whoopie pie pans with nonstick cooking spray. Cut small rounds of parchment paper to fit bottoms of cups in whoopie pie pans. Line cups with parchment rounds; spray parchment with cooking spray. Sift flour and baking powder into medium bowl.

2. Combine milk, butter and vanilla in small saucepan; heat over low heat until butter is melted. Beat eggs and granulated sugar in large bowl with electric mixer at high speed until mixture is pale yellow and triples in volume.

3. Gently fold warm milk mixture into egg mixture. Add flour mixture to egg mixture in four parts, beating at low speed after each addition until batter is smooth. Spoon 3 tablespoonfuls of batter into each prepared whoopie pie cup.

4. Bake 10 to 12 minutes or until cookies spring back when lightly touched. Cool 5 minutes in pans. Remove to wire racks; cool completely.

5. For filling, beat cream in large bowl with electric mixer at high speed 3 minutes or until soft peaks form. Gradually add powdered sugar; beat about 2 minutes or until stiff peaks form. Beat in vanilla.

6. Stir jelly in small bowl until thinned and smooth; spread on flat sides of cookies. Spread scant 3 tablespoons whipped cream over jam on half of cookies; top with remaining cookies.   *Makes 12 whoopie pies*

CHOCOLATE BLISS

Double Chocolate-Peanut Butter Whoopie Pies

Cookies
- 1⅔ cups all-purpose flour
- ⅔ cup unsweetened cocoa powder
- 1½ teaspoons baking soda
- ½ teaspoon salt
- 1 cup granulated sugar
- ½ cup (1 stick) butter, softened
- 2 eggs
- 1½ teaspoons vanilla
- ¾ cup milk
- ¾ cup semisweet chocolate chips

Filling
- 1 cup peanut butter
- ½ stick (¼ cup) butter, softened
- 1½ cups powdered sugar
- 2 tablespoons milk

1. For cookies, preheat oven to 350°F. Line two cookie sheets with parchment paper. Sift flour, cocoa, baking soda and salt into medium bowl.

2. Beat granulated sugar and ½ cup butter in large bowl with electric mixer at medium speed 5 minutes or until light and fluffy. Add eggs, one at a time, beating well after each addition. Beat in vanilla. Add half of flour mixture and ½ cup milk; beat until blended. Beat in remaining flour mixture, ¼ cup milk and chocolate chips until smooth. Drop rounded tablespoonfuls of batter 2 inches apart onto prepared cookie sheets.

3. Bake 10 to 12 minutes or until cookies spring back when lightly touched. Cool 2 minutes on cookie sheets. Remove to wire racks; cool completely.

4. For filling, beat peanut butter and ¼ cup butter in large bowl with electric mixer at medium speed until creamy. Add powdered sugar and 2 tablespoons milk; beat until smooth.

5. Pipe or spread 2 tablespoons filling on flat side of half of cookies; top with remaining cookies. *Makes 18 whoopie pies*

Chocolate Cookies & Cream Whoopie Pies

Cookies

- 1⅔ cups all-purpose flour
- ⅔ cup unsweetened cocoa powder
- 1½ teaspoons baking soda
- ½ teaspoon salt
- 1 cup granulated sugar
- ½ cup (1 stick) butter, softened
- 2 eggs
- 1½ teaspoons vanilla
- 1 cup vanilla Greek yogurt

Filling

- 2 cups powdered sugar
- ¾ cup (1½ sticks) butter, softened
- 10 cream-filled chocolate sandwich cookies, crushed

1. For cookies, preheat oven to 350°F. Line two cookie sheets with parchment paper. Sift flour, cocoa, baking soda and salt into medium bowl.

2. Beat granulated sugar and ½ cup butter in large bowl with electric mixer at medium speed 5 minutes or until light and fluffy. Add eggs, one at a time, beating well after each addition. Beat in vanilla. Add half of flour mixture and ½ cup yogurt; beat just until blended. Beat in remaining flour mixture and ½ cup yogurt until smooth. Drop rounded tablespoonfuls of batter 2 inches apart onto prepared cookie sheets.

3. Bake 10 to 12 minutes or until cookies spring back when lightly touched. Cool 2 minutes on cookie sheets. Remove to wire racks; cool completely.

4. For filling, beat powdered sugar and ¾ cup butter in large bowl with electric mixer at medium speed until light and fluffy. Beat in crushed cookies at low speed until blended.

5. Spread 2 tablespoons filling on flat side of half of cookies; top with remaining cookies. *Makes 18 whoopie pies*

Black & White Whoopie Pies

Cookies
2⅔ cups all-purpose flour
2 teaspoons baking powder
1 teaspoon baking soda
½ teaspoon salt
1¼ cups granulated sugar
¾ cup (1½ sticks) butter, softened
2 eggs
1 teaspoon vanilla
½ cup milk
3 ounces bittersweet chocolate, melted and cooled

Filling
2 cups powdered sugar
2 cups marshmallow creme
1 cup (2 sticks) butter, softened
2 teaspoons vanilla

1. For cookies, preheat oven to 350°F. Line two cookie sheets with parchment paper. Combine flour, baking powder, baking soda and salt in medium bowl.

2. Beat granulated sugar and ¾ cup butter in large bowl with electric mixer at medium speed 5 minutes or until light and fluffy. Beat in eggs and 1 teaspoon vanilla until blended. Add flour mixture alternately with milk, beginning and ending with flour mixture; beat just until blended.

3. Remove half of dough to medium bowl; stir in melted chocolate just until blended. Drop 3 level tablespoonfuls of chocolate batter 3 inches apart onto prepared cookie sheets.

4. Bake 12 to 13 minutes or until centers spring back when lightly touched. Cool 5 minutes on cookie sheets. Remove to wire racks; cool completely. Repeat with vanilla batter.

5. For filling, beat powdered sugar, marshmallow creme, 1 cup butter and 2 teaspoons vanilla in large bowl with electric mixer at medium speed about 2 minutes or until light and fluffy.

6. Pipe or spread about 3 tablespoons filling on flat side of chocolate cookies; top with vanilla cookies.   *Makes 12 whoopie pies*

Mint Chocolate Whoopie Pies

Cookies

- 2 cups all-purpose flour
- ¼ cup plus 1 tablespoon unsweetened cocoa powder
- 1 teaspoon baking powder
- 1 teaspoon baking soda
- ½ teaspoon salt
- 1 cup granulated sugar
- ½ cup (1 stick) butter, softened
- 1 egg
- 1 egg yolk
- 1 tablespoon vanilla
- 1 cup milk

Filling

- 8 ounces bittersweet or semisweet chocolate chips
- ½ cup whipping cream
- ¾ cup (1½ sticks) plus 2 tablespoons butter, softened, divided
- 2½ cups powdered sugar
- 1 teaspoon peppermint extract
- ⅛ teaspoon salt
- 3 to 4 drops liquid green food coloring

1. For cookies, preheat oven to 350°F. Line two cookie sheets with parchment paper. Sift flour, cocoa, baking powder, baking soda and ½ teaspoon salt into medium bowl.

2. Beat granulated sugar and ½ cup butter in large bowl with electric mixer at medium speed 5 minutes or until fluffy. Add egg, egg yolk and vanilla, beating until well blended. Add half of flour mixture and ½ cup milk; beat until blended. Beat in remaining flour mixture and ½ cup milk until smooth. Drop rounded tablespoonfuls of batter 2 inches apart onto prepared cookie sheets.

3. Bake 10 to 12 minutes or until cookies spring back when lightly touched. Cool 2 minutes on cookie sheets. Remove to wire racks; cool completely.

4. For filling, place chocolate chips in medium bowl. Bring cream and 2 tablespoons butter to a simmer in small saucepan; pour over chocolate and let stand until chocolate begins to melt. Stir until smooth. Let stand 15 minutes or until thick and spreadable.

5. Beat remaining ¾ cup butter in large bowl with electric mixer at medium speed until light and fluffy. Add powdered sugar, peppermint extract, ⅛ teaspoon salt and food coloring; beat until smooth.

6. Spread scant tablespoon chocolate filling on flat side of half of cookies. Spread or pipe 2 tablespoons mint filling on flat side of remaining cookies. Make sandwiches.   *Makes 22 whoopie pies*

Pumpkin Chocolate Chip Whoopie Pies

Cookies
- 2 cups all-purpose flour
- 2 teaspoons ground cinnamon
- 1 teaspoon baking soda
- 1 teaspoon ground cloves
- ½ teaspoon salt
- 1 cup (2 sticks) butter, softened
- ½ cup granulated sugar
- ½ cup packed brown sugar
- 1 cup canned solid-pack pumpkin
- 1 egg
- 2 teaspoons vanilla
- 2 cups semisweet chocolate chips

Filling
- 1 cup (2 sticks) butter, softened
- 2 teaspoons vanilla
- 4 cups powdered sugar
- ¼ cup evaporated milk

1. Preheat oven to 350°F. Line two cookie sheets with parchment paper. Combine flour, cinnamon, baking soda, cloves and salt in small bowl.

2. Beat 1 cup butter, granulated sugar and brown sugar in large bowl with electric mixer at medium speed about 5 minutes or until light and fluffy. Add pumpkin, egg and 2 teaspoons vanilla; beat 2 minutes or until blended. Gradually add flour mixture, beating at low speed just until blended. Stir in chocolate chips. Drop rounded tablespoonfuls of batter 2 inches apart onto prepared cookie sheets.

3. Bake 11 to 14 minutes or until centers are set. Cool 2 minutes on cookie sheets. Remove to wire racks; cool completely.

4. For filling, beat 1 cup butter and 2 teaspoons vanilla in large bowl with electric mixer at medium speed until creamy. Add powdered sugar, 1 cup at a time, beating well after each addition. Add evaporated milk; beat until light and fluffy.

5. Spread 2 rounded tablespoons filling on flat side of half of cookies; top with remaining cookies.   *Makes 24 whoopie pies*

German Chocolate Whoopie Pies

Cookies

    2 cups all-purpose flour
    ½ cup unsweetened cocoa powder
    1½ teaspoons baking soda
    1 teaspoon salt
    1 cup packed brown sugar
    ½ cup (1 stick) butter, softened
    1 egg
    2 teaspoons vanilla
    1 cup buttermilk

Filling

    3 egg yolks
    ¾ cup evaporated milk
    ½ cup (1 stick) butter
    ½ cup granulated sugar
    ½ cup packed brown sugar
    1½ cups sweetened shredded coconut
    1 cup chopped pecans
    1 teaspoon vanilla

1. For cookies, preheat oven to 350°F. Line two cookie sheets with parchment paper. Combine flour, cocoa, baking soda and salt in medium bowl.

2. Beat 1 cup brown sugar and ½ cup butter in large bowl with electric mixer at medium speed about 5 minutes or until light and fluffy. Beat in egg and 2 teaspoons vanilla until blended. Alternately beat in flour mixture and buttermilk at low speed, beginning and ending with flour mixture. Drop rounded tablespoonfuls of batter 2 inches apart onto prepared cookie sheets.

3. Bake 14 to 16 minutes or until cookies spring back when lightly touched. Cool 10 minutes on cookie sheets. Remove to wire racks; cool completely.

4. For filling, beat egg yolks lightly in small bowl. Combine evaporated milk, ½ cup butter, granulated sugar and ½ cup brown sugar in medium saucepan; bring to a boil over medium heat, stirring constantly. Remove from heat; whisk ⅓ cup hot milk mixture into egg yolks. Whisk egg yolk mixture back into milk mixture in saucepan; bring to a boil, stirring constantly. Boil gently over medium-low heat 1 minute, stirring constantly. Remove from heat; stir in coconut, pecans and 1 teaspoon vanilla. Cool about 30 minutes or until mixture is thick and spreadable, stirring frequently.

5. Spread 2 tablespoons filling on flat side of half of cookies; top with remaining cookies.   *Makes 24 whoopie pies*

Chocolate & Salted Caramel Whoopie Pies

Cookies

1⅔ cups all-purpose flour
⅔ cup unsweetened cocoa powder
1½ teaspoons baking soda
½ teaspoon salt
1 cup granulated sugar
½ cup (1 stick) butter, softened
1 egg
1½ teaspoons vanilla
1 cup milk

Filling

1 cup granulated sugar
¾ cup whipping cream
¾ cup (1½ sticks) butter, softened, divided
¾ teaspoon coarse salt
4 ounces cream cheese, softened
2½ cups powdered sugar

1. For cookies, preheat oven to 350°F. Line two cookie sheets with parchment paper. Sift flour, cocoa, baking soda and ½ teaspoon salt into medium bowl.

2. Beat 1 cup granulated sugar and ½ cup butter in large bowl with electric mixer at medium speed 5 minutes or until light and fluffy. Beat in egg and vanilla. Add half of flour mixture and ½ cup milk; beat at low speed until combined. Beat in remaining flour mixture and milk until smooth. Drop rounded tablespoonfuls of batter 2 inches apart onto prepared cookie sheets.

3. Bake 10 to 12 minutes or until cookies spring back when lightly touched. Cool 2 minutes on cookie sheets. Remove to wire racks; cool completely.

4. For filling, heat 1 cup granulated sugar in medium heavy saucepan over medium-high heat, without stirring, until amber in color. Remove from heat. Carefully stir in cream, ¼ cup butter and coarse salt (mixture will foam). Let stand 15 minutes or until caramel cools to room temperature.

5. Beat remaining ½ cup butter and cream cheese in large bowl with electric mixer at medium speed until creamy. Beat in ½ cup caramel until blended. Beat in powdered sugar until light and fluffy.

6. Pipe or spread 2 tablespoons filling on flat side of half of cookies; top with remaining cookies. Drizzle with remaining caramel, if desired.

Makes 20 whoopie pies

Whoopie Pies

Cookies

    1 package (about 18 ounces) devil's food cake mix *without* pudding in the mix
    1 package (4-serving size) chocolate instant pudding and pie filling mix
    4 eggs
    1 cup water
    ½ cup (1 stick) butter, softened

Filling

    1¼ cups marshmallow creme
    ¾ cup (1½ sticks) butter, softened
    ¾ cup powdered sugar
    ½ teaspoon vanilla

1. For cookies, preheat oven to 350°F. Grease two cookie sheets or line with parchment paper.

2. Beat cake mix, pudding mix, eggs, water and ½ cup butter in large bowl with electric mixer at low speed just until moistened. Beat at medium speed about 2 minutes or until light and thick. Drop heaping tablespoonfuls of batter 2 inches apart onto prepared cookie sheets.

3. Bake 12 to 14 minutes or until cookies spring back when lightly touched. Cool 5 minutes on cookie sheets. Remove to wire racks; cool completely.

4. For filling, beat marshmallow creme, ¾ cup butter, powdered sugar and vanilla in large bowl with electric mixer at high speed 2 minutes or until light and fluffy.

5. Pipe or spread filling on flat side of half of cookies; top with remaining cookies.

Makes 24 whoopie pies

Chocolate-Almond Whoopie Pies

Cookies
- 1½ cups all-purpose flour
- ½ cup almond meal
- ¾ teaspoon baking powder
- ¼ teaspoon baking soda
- ¼ teaspoon salt
- 1 cup packed brown sugar
- ½ cup (1 stick) butter, softened
- 2 eggs
- 2 tablespoons whipping cream
- 2 teaspoons almond extract
- 1 teaspoon vanilla

Filling
- 10 ounces semisweet chocolate chips
- 2 tablespoons butter
- ¾ cup whipping cream
- ½ cup powdered sugar

1. For cookies, preheat oven to 350°F. Line two cookie sheets with parchment paper. Combine flour, almond meal, baking powder, baking soda and salt in medium bowl.

2. Beat brown sugar and ½ cup butter in large bowl with electric mixer at medium speed 5 minutes or until light and fluffy. Add eggs, one at a time, beating well after each addition. Beat in 2 tablespoons cream, almond extract and vanilla. Add flour mixture; beat at low speed just until blended. Drop rounded tablespoonfuls of batter 2 inches apart onto prepared cookie sheets.

3. Bake 10 to 12 minutes or until cookies spring back when lightly touched. Cool 2 minutes on cookie sheets. Remove to wire racks; cool completely.

4. For filling, place chocolate chips and 2 tablespoons butter in medium bowl. Bring ¾ cup cream to a simmer in small saucepan; pour over chocolate. Let stand 5 minutes; stir until smooth. Whisk in powdered sugar until blended; let stand until filling thickens to desired consistency.

5. Pipe or spread 2 tablespoons filling on flat side of half of cookies; top with remaining cookies. *Makes 18 whoopie pies*

Mocha Whoopie Pies

Cookies

- 1⅔ cups all-purpose flour
- 1½ teaspoons baking soda
- ½ teaspoon salt
- ¾ cup hot coffee
- ⅔ cup unsweetened cocoa powder
- 2 tablespoons instant espresso powder
- 1 cup granulated sugar
- ½ cup (1 stick) butter, softened
- 1 egg
- 1½ teaspoons vanilla

Filling

- 2 cups powdered sugar
- ¾ cup (1½ sticks) butter, softened
- 1 tablespoon instant espresso powder dissolved in 2 tablespoons hot water
- 1½ teaspoons vanilla

1. For cookies, preheat oven to 350°F. Line two cookie sheets with parchment paper. Sift flour, baking soda and salt into medium bowl. Whisk coffee, cocoa and 2 tablespoons espresso powder in 2-cup measure until blended; cool to room temperature.

2. Beat granulated sugar and ½ cup butter in large bowl with electric mixer at medium speed 5 minutes or until light and fluffy. Beat in egg and 1½ teaspoons vanilla. Add half of flour mixture and half of coffee mixture; beat just until blended. Beat in remaining flour mixture and coffee mixture until smooth. Drop rounded tablespoonfuls of batter 2 inches apart onto prepared cookie sheets.

3. Bake 10 to 12 minutes or until cookies spring back when lightly touched. Cool 2 minutes on cookie sheets. Remove to wire racks; cool completely.

4. For filling, beat powdered sugar and ¾ cup butter in large bowl with electric mixer at medium speed 5 minutes or until light and fluffy. Add espresso mixture and 1½ teaspoons vanilla; beat until smooth.

5. Pipe or spread 2 tablespoons filling on flat side of half of cookies; top with remaining cookies. *Makes 20 whoopie pies*

Chocolate Chip Whoopie Pies

Cookies
- 2¼ cups all-purpose flour
- 1½ teaspoons baking powder
- ½ teaspoon salt
- ½ cup (1 stick) butter, softened
- ½ cup granulated sugar
- ½ cup packed brown sugar
- 2 eggs
- ½ cup buttermilk
- 2 tablespoons evaporated milk
- 1 teaspoon baking soda
- 1 teaspoon white vinegar
- 1 teaspoon vanilla
- 1 cup semisweet chocolate chips

Filling
- 2⅔ cups powdered sugar
- 1 cup unsweetened cocoa powder
- 1 cup (2 sticks) butter, softened
- ½ cup whipping cream
- 2 teaspoons vanilla
- 1 teaspoon salt

1. For cookies, preheat oven to 375°F. Line two cookie sheets with parchment paper. Combine flour, baking powder and salt in medium bowl.

2. Beat ½ cup butter, granulated sugar and brown sugar in large bowl with electric mixer at medium speed 5 minutes or until light and fluffy. Add eggs and buttermilk; beat until blended (mixture may look curdled).

3. Whisk evaporated milk, baking soda and vinegar in small bowl. Add to butter mixture with flour mixture; beat at low speed just until blended. Add 1 teaspoon vanilla; beat at medium speed about 1 minute or until batter is well blended and light. Stir in chocolate chips. Drop heaping tablespoonfuls of batter 2 inches apart onto prepared cookie sheets.

4. Bake 10 to 12 minutes or until edges begin to brown. Cool 5 minutes on cookie sheets. Remove to wire racks; cool completely.

5. For filling, sift powdered sugar and cocoa into medium bowl. Beat 1 cup butter in large bowl with electric mixer at medium speed until creamy. Add powdered sugar mixture; beat until crumbly. Add cream, 2 teaspoons vanilla and salt; beat at high speed about 3 minutes or until smooth and fluffy.

6. Pipe or spread filling on flat side of half of cookies; top with remaining cookies.

Makes 24 whoopie pies

Chocolate Peppermint Whoopie Pies

Cookies

1⅔ cups all-purpose flour
⅔ cup unsweetened cocoa powder
1½ teaspoons baking soda
½ teaspoon salt
1 cup packed brown sugar
½ cup (1 stick) butter, softened
1 egg
1½ teaspoons vanilla
1 cup milk

Filling

¾ cup (1½ sticks) butter, softened
3 cups powdered sugar
2 tablespoons milk
1 teaspoon peppermint extract
6 candy canes, crushed

1. For cookies, preheat oven to 350°F. Line two cookie sheets with parchment paper. Sift flour, cocoa, baking soda and salt into medium bowl.

2. Beat brown sugar and ½ cup butter in large bowl with electric mixer at medium speed 5 minutes or until light and fluffy. Beat in egg and vanilla. Beat in half of flour mixture and ½ cup milk until blended. Beat in remaining flour mixture and ½ cup milk until smooth. Drop ¼ cupfuls of batter 2 inches apart onto prepared cookie sheets.

3. Bake 10 to 12 minutes or until cookies spring back when lightly touched. Cool 2 minutes on cookie sheets. Remove to wire racks; cool completely.

4. For filling, beat ¾ cup butter in large bowl with electric mixer at medium speed until creamy. Alternately beat in powdered sugar and 2 tablespoons milk, beating until well blended after each addition. Beat in peppermint extract until smooth.

5. Spread 2 tablespoons filling on flat side of half of cookies; top with remaining cookies. Place crushed candy in shallow dish; roll edges of cookies in candy.

Makes 10 whoopie pies

PARTY PLEASERS

Pink Lemonade Whoopie Pies

Cookies
- 1 package (about 18 ounces) white cake mix
- ½ cup water
- ⅓ cup vegetable oil
- 3 tablespoons powdered pink lemonade mix
- 1 egg
- 1 teaspoon grated lemon peel
- Pink decorating sugar or pink sprinkles

Filling
- 3 tablespoons powdered pink lemonade mix
- 2 tablespoons lemon juice
- 1 cup (2 sticks) butter, softened
- 3 cups powdered sugar
- Pink food coloring (optional)

1. For cookies, preheat oven to 350°F. Line two cookie sheets with parchment paper.

2. Combine cake mix, water, oil, 3 tablespoons lemonade mix, egg and lemon peel in large bowl; mix with wooden spoon until well blended.

3. Drop tablespoonfuls of batter 2 inches apart onto prepared cookie sheets. Sprinkle generously with pink sugar.

4. Bake 12 minutes or until set. Cool 5 minutes on cookie sheets. Remove to wire racks; cool completely.

5. For filling, stir 3 tablespoons lemonade mix and lemon juice in large bowl until blended. Add butter; beat with electric mixer at medium-high speed until creamy. Add powdered sugar and food coloring, if desired; beat until light and fluffy.

6. Pipe or spread filling on flat sides of half of cookies; top with remaining cookies. *Makes 11 whoopie pies*

Pumpkin Pecan Pie Sandwiches

Cookies

    2 cups all-purpose flour
    2 teaspoons baking powder
    1 teaspoon baking soda
    1 teaspoon ground cinnamon
    1 teaspoon ground ginger
    ¾ teaspoon salt
    ½ teaspoon ground nutmeg
    ¼ teaspoon black pepper (optional)
    ⅛ teaspoon ground cloves
    1 cup packed brown sugar
    ½ cup (1 stick) butter, softened
    ⅓ cup granulated sugar
    2 eggs
    ¼ cup buttermilk
    1 teaspoon vanilla
    1 cup canned solid-pack pumpkin

Filling

    3 tablespoons butter
    ½ cup packed brown sugar
    ½ cup light corn syrup
    ¼ teaspoon salt
    ¼ teaspoon vanilla
    1½ cups coarsely chopped pecans

1. For cookies, preheat oven to 350°F. Line two cookie sheets with parchment paper. Sift flour, baking powder, baking soda, cinnamon, ginger, ¾ teaspoon salt, nutmeg, pepper, if desired, and cloves into medium bowl.

2. Beat 1 cup brown sugar, ½ cup butter and granulated sugar in large bowl with electric mixer at medium speed 5 minutes or until light and fluffy. Add eggs, one at a time, beating well after each addition. Beat in 1 teaspoon vanilla. Alternately beat in flour mixture and buttermilk, beginning and ending with flour mixture. Beat in pumpkin until smooth. Drop rounded tablespoonfuls of batter 2 inches apart onto prepared cookie sheets.

3. Bake 10 to 12 minutes or until cookies spring back when lightly touched. Cool 2 minutes on cookie sheets. Remove to wire racks; cool completely.

4. For filling, melt 3 tablespoons butter in small saucepan over medium heat. Stir in ½ cup brown sugar, corn syrup, ¼ teaspoon salt and ¼ teaspoon vanilla until smooth; cook until hot, stirring frequently. Stir in pecans; let cool.

5. Spread 2 tablespoons filling on flat side of half of cookies; top with remaining cookies. *Makes 26 whoopie pies*

Mocha-Eggnog Whoopie Pies

Cookies

- 2 cups all-purpose flour
- 1½ teaspoons baking soda
- ½ teaspoon salt
- ½ teaspoon ground nutmeg
- ½ teaspoon ground cinnamon
- 1 cup granulated sugar
- ½ cup (1 stick) butter, softened
- 1 egg
- 1½ teaspoons vanilla
- 1 cup eggnog

Filling

- 2 cups powdered sugar
- ¾ cup (1½ sticks) butter, softened
- ¼ cup unsweetened cocoa powder
- 2 teaspoons instant espresso powder dissolved in 1 tablespoon hot water

1. For cookies, preheat oven to 350°F. Line two cookie sheets with parchment paper. Sift flour, baking soda, salt, nutmeg and cinnamon into medium bowl.

2. Beat granulated sugar and ½ cup butter in large bowl with electric mixer at medium speed 5 minutes or until light and fluffy. Beat in egg and vanilla. Add half of flour mixture and ½ cup eggnog; beat just until combined. Beat in remaining flour mixture and ½ cup eggnog until smooth. Drop rounded tablespoonfuls of batter 2 inches apart onto prepared cookie sheets.

3. Bake 10 to 12 minutes or until cookies spring back when lightly touched. Cool 2 minutes on cookie sheets. Remove to wire racks; cool completely.

4. For filling, beat powdered sugar and ¾ cup butter in large bowl with electric mixer at medium speed until fluffy. Add cocoa and espresso mixture; beat until smooth.

5. Pipe or spread 2 tablespoons filling on flat side of half of cookies; top with remaining cookies.   *Makes 22 whoopie pies*

Whoopie Pies with Mascarpone Filling

Cookies
- 1¾ cups all-purpose flour
- ¾ cup unsweetened cocoa powder
- 1½ teaspoons baking soda
- ½ teaspoon baking powder
- ½ teaspoon salt
- 1 cup packed brown sugar
- ½ cup (1 stick) butter, softened
- 1 cup buttermilk
- 1 egg
- 1 teaspoon vanilla

Filling
- 8 ounces mascarpone cheese
- 8 ounces ricotta cheese, drained
- ¼ cup plus 2 tablespoons powdered sugar
- 1 teaspoon vanilla

1. For cookies, sift flour, cocoa, baking soda, baking powder and salt into medium bowl.

2. Beat brown sugar and butter in large bowl with electric mixer at medium-high speed about 3 minutes or until light and fluffy. Add buttermilk, egg and 1 teaspoon vanilla; beat 2 minutes or until well blended. (Mixture will look curdled.) Gradually add flour mixture, beating at low speed just until blended. Cover and refrigerate 1 to 2 hours.

3. Preheat oven to 375°F. Line two cookie sheets with parchment paper. Drop 2 tablespoonfuls of batter 2 inches apart onto prepared cookie sheets.

4. Bake 9 minutes or until cookies are puffed and cracked on top. Cool 10 minutes on cookie sheets. Remove to wire racks; cool completely.

5. For filling, combine mascarpone, ricotta, powdered sugar and 2 teaspoons vanilla in medium bowl; mix well.

6. Spread 2 tablespoons filling on flat side of half of cookies; top with remaining cookies. *Makes 11 whoopie pies*

Gingerbread Whoopie Pies

Cookies

- 2 cups all-purpose flour
- 1½ teaspoons ground ginger
- 1 teaspoon ground cinnamon
- ¾ teaspoon baking soda
- ¾ teaspoon salt
- ⅛ teaspoon ground nutmeg
- ¾ cup packed dark brown sugar
- ½ cup (1 stick) butter, softened
- ¼ cup molasses
- 1 egg
- 1 teaspoon vanilla
- ¼ cup turbinado sugar

Filling

- 1 jar (7 ounces) marshmallow creme
- 4 ounces cream cheese, softened
- ¼ cup (½ stick) butter, softened
- 1 teaspoon vanilla
- 3 tablespoons chopped walnuts

1. For cookies, preheat oven to 350°F. Line two cookie sheets with parchment paper. Sift flour, ginger, cinnamon, baking soda, salt and nutmeg into medium bowl.

2. Beat brown sugar and ½ cup butter in large bowl with electric mixer at medium speed 5 minutes or until light and fluffy. Add molasses, egg and 1 teaspoon vanilla, beating until well blended. Beat in flour mixture until blended. Drop rounded tablespoonfuls of batter 2 inches apart onto prepared cookie sheets. Sprinkle with turbinado sugar and gently press with bottom of glass.

3. Bake 10 to 12 minutes or until cookies spring back when lightly touched. Cool 2 minutes on cookie sheets. Remove to wire racks; cool completely.

4. For filling, beat marshmallow creme, cream cheese and ¼ cup butter in large bowl with electric mixer at medium speed until light and fluffy. Add 1 teaspoon vanilla; beat until smooth.

5. Pipe or spread 2 tablespoons filling on flat side of half of cookies; top with remaining cookies. Sprinkle with walnuts.   *Makes 18 whoopie pies*

Maple-Bourbon Whoopie Pies

Cookies
- 1¼ cups all-purpose flour
- ½ teaspoon baking soda
- ¼ teaspoon salt
- ½ cup buttermilk
- 3 tablespoons maple syrup
- ½ teaspoon vanilla
- ½ cup granulated sugar
- ¼ cup (½ stick) butter, softened
- ⅓ cup finely chopped pecans

Filling
- 1½ cups powdered sugar
- 4 ounces cream cheese, softened
- 2 tablespoons butter, softened
- ½ tablespoon bourbon
- ½ teaspoon vanilla

1. For cookies, preheat oven to 350°F. Line two cookie sheets with parchment paper. Combine flour, baking soda and salt in medium bowl. Combine buttermilk, maple syrup and ½ teaspoon vanilla in small bowl.

2. Beat granulated sugar and ¼ cup butter in large bowl with electric mixer at medium speed 1 minute or until well blended. Alternately add flour mixture and buttermilk mixture, beating at low speed after each addition until well blended. Stir in pecans. Drop 2 level tablespoonfuls of batter 2 inches apart onto prepared cookie sheets.

3. Bake 11 to 13 minutes or until edges are golden brown. Cool 10 minutes on cookie sheets. Remove to wire racks; cool completely.

4. For filling, beat powdered sugar, cream cheese and 2 tablespoons butter in large bowl with electric mixer at medium speed 2 minutes or until smooth. Add bourbon and ½ teaspoon vanilla; beat 1 minute.

5. Pipe or spread filling on flat side of half of cookies; top with remaining cookies. *Makes 10 whoopie pies*

Lemon Ricotta Whoopie Pies

Cookies

  2 cups all-purpose flour
  2 teaspoons baking powder
  1 cup granulated sugar
  ½ cup (1 stick) butter, softened
  2 eggs
  ⅔ cup ricotta cheese
     Grated peel of 2 lemons
  2 tablespoons fresh lemon juice

Filling

  ¾ cup (1½ sticks) butter, softened
  3 cups powdered sugar
  ¼ cup milk
  1½ teaspoons vanilla

1. For cookies, preheat oven to 350°F. Line two cookie sheets with parchment paper. Sift flour and baking powder into medium bowl.

2. Beat granulated sugar and ½ cup butter in large bowl with electric mixer at medium speed 5 minutes or until light and fluffy. Add eggs, one at a time, beating well after each addition. Add half of flour mixture and half of ricotta; beat until combined. Beat in remaining flour mixture and ricotta until well blended. Beat in lemon peel and lemon juice until smooth. Drop rounded tablespoonfuls of batter 2 inches apart onto prepared cookie sheets.

3. Bake 10 to 12 minutes or until cookies spring back when lightly touched. Cool 2 minutes on cookie sheets. Remove to wire racks; cool completely.

4. For filling, beat ¾ cup butter in large bowl with electric mixer at medium speed until fluffy. Add powdered sugar, milk and vanilla; beat until smooth.

5. Spread 2 tablespoons filling on flat side of half of cookies; top with remaining cookies.   *Makes 20 whoopie pies*

Sweet Potato Spice Whoopie Pies

Cookies

1½ pounds sweet potatoes, quartered
1½ cups all-purpose flour
1¼ cups granulated sugar
2 teaspoons baking powder
1 teaspoon ground cinnamon
½ teaspoon baking soda
½ teaspoon salt
¼ teaspoon ground allspice
¾ cup canola oil
2 eggs
1 teaspoon vanilla
½ cup chopped walnuts

Filling

1 package (8 ounces) cream cheese, softened
¼ cup (½ stick) butter, softened
1½ cups powdered sugar
¼ teaspoon salt
¼ teaspoon vanilla

1. For cookies, place sweet potato in large saucepan; add enough water to cover. Cover and cook over medium heat 30 minutes or until fork-tender, adding additional water if necessary. Drain and set aside until cool enough to handle. Peel and mash sweet potatoes; measure 2 cups.

2. Preheat oven to 350°F. Line two cookie sheets with parchment paper. Sift flour, granulated sugar, baking powder, cinnamon, baking soda, ½ teaspoon salt and allspice into medium bowl.

3. Beat mashed sweet potatoes, oil, eggs and 1 teaspoon vanilla in large bowl with electric mixer at low speed until blended. Add flour mixture; beat at medium speed until well blended. Stir in walnuts. Drop rounded tablespoonfuls of batter 2 inches apart onto prepared cookie sheets.

4. Bake 10 to 12 minutes or until cookies spring back when lightly touched. Cool 2 minutes on cookie sheets. Remove to wire racks; cool completely.

5. For filling, beat cream cheese and butter in large bowl with electric mixer at medium speed until creamy. Add powdered sugar, ¼ teaspoon salt and ¼ teaspoon vanilla; beat until smooth.

6. Pipe or spread 2 tablespoons filling on flat side of half of cookies; top with remaining cookies.   *Makes 22 whoopie pies*

Wooly Spider Whoopie Pies

Cookies
- 2 cups all-purpose flour
- ½ cup unsweetened cocoa powder
- 1¼ teaspoons baking soda
- 1 teaspoon salt
- 1 cup packed brown sugar
- ½ cup (1 stick) butter, softened
- 1 egg
- 1 teaspoon vanilla
- 1 cup buttermilk

Filling
- 2 cups marshmallow creme
- 1¼ cups powdered sugar
- ½ cup (1 stick) butter, softened
- 2 tablespoons unsweetened cocoa powder
- 1 teaspoon vanilla
- 1 cup semisweet chocolate chips
- ⅓ cup chocolate sprinkles
- 12 candy-coated chocolate pieces
- 48 (2-inch) pieces black string licorice

1. For cookies, preheat oven to 350°F. Line two cookie sheets with parchment paper. Sift flour, ½ cup cocoa, baking soda and salt into medium bowl.

2. Beat brown sugar, ½ cup butter, egg and 1 teaspoon vanilla in large bowl with electric mixer at medium speed until blended. Alternately add flour mixture and buttermilk, beating at low speed after each addition until smooth and well blended. Drop scant ¼ cupfuls of batter 2 inches apart onto prepared cookie sheets.

3. Bake 12 minutes or until puffed and tops spring back when lightly touched. Cool 10 minutes on cookie sheets. Remove to wire racks; cool completely.

4. For filling, beat marshmallow creme, powdered sugar, ½ cup butter, 2 tablespoons cocoa and 1 teaspoon vanilla in large bowl with electric mixer at medium speed until smooth.

5. Place chocolate chips in small microwavable bowl; microwave on HIGH 1 minute. Stir; microwave at 15-second intervals, stirring after each interval, until chocolate is melted.

6. Spread melted chocolate on tops of six cookies; cover with sprinkles and add chocolate pieces for eyes. Spread flat sides of remaining six cookies with filling; top with chocolate-covered cookies. Press licorice pieces into filling for legs. *Makes 6 whoopie pies*

Orange Harvey Wallbanger Whoopie Pies

Cookies

    1 package (about 18 ounces) vanilla cake mix *without* pudding in the mix
    1 package (4-serving size) vanilla instant pudding and pie filling mix
    4 eggs
    ¾ cup orange juice
    ½ cup vegetable oil
    1 teaspoon orange extract

Filling

    1 package (8 ounces) cream cheese, softened
    ¼ cup (½ stick) butter, softened
    2 tablespoons orange juice
    2 tablespoons vodka
    2 tablespoons Galliano
    2 teaspoons grated orange peel
    1 teaspoon vanilla
   1¼ cups powdered sugar

1. For cookies, preheat oven to 325°F. Line two cookie sheets with parchment paper.

2. Beat cake mix, pudding mix, eggs, ¾ cup orange juice, oil and orange extract in large bowl with electric mixer at low speed 30 seconds or until blended. Beat at medium speed 2 minutes. Drop rounded tablespoonfuls of batter 2 inches apart onto prepared cookie sheets.

3. Bake 10 to 12 minutes or until centers are set. Cool 10 minutes on cookie sheets. Remove to wire racks; cool completely.

4. For filling, beat cream cheese, butter, 2 tablespoons orange juice, vodka, Galliano, orange peel and vanilla in large bowl with electic mixer at medium speed until creamy. Add powdered sugar; beat 2 minutes or until light and fluffy.

5. Spread 2 tablespoons filling on flat side of half of cookies; top with remaining cookies. *Makes 26 whoopie pies*

Mini Confetti Whoopie Pies

Cookies

- 2 cups all-purpose flour
- 1 teaspoon baking soda
- 1 teaspoon baking powder
- ½ teaspoon salt
- ½ cup granulated sugar
- ½ cup packed brown sugar
- ½ cup vegetable oil
- 1 egg
- 1 teaspoon vanilla
- ½ cup plain Greek yogurt
- ½ cup milk
- 1 tablespoon rainbow sprinkles

Filling

- 2 cups powdered sugar
- 1 cup (2 sticks) butter, softened
- 2 tablespoons plain Greek yogurt
- 1 teaspoon vanilla
- 2 tablespoons rainbow sprinkles

1. For cookies, preheat oven to 350°F. Line two cookie sheets with parchment paper. Combine flour, baking soda, baking powder and salt in medium bowl.

2. Combine granulated sugar, brown sugar, oil, egg and 1 teaspoon vanilla in large bowl; stir until well blended. Add ½ cup yogurt, milk and flour mixture; stir just until blended.

3. Drop half teaspoonfuls of batter 2 inches apart on cookie sheets. Sprinkle with 1 tablespoon sprinkles.

4. Bake 8 minutes or until lightly browned around edges. Remove to wire racks; cool completely.

5. For filling, beat powdered sugar, butter, 2 tablespoons yogurt and 1 teaspoon vanilla in large bowl with electric mixer at medium speed until light and fluffy.

6. Spread filling on flat side of half of cookies; top with remaining cookies. Place 2 tablespoons sprinkles in shallow dish; roll edges of cookies in sprinkles.   *Makes 40 mini whoopie pies*

Pumpkin Spiced Whoopie Pies

Cookies
2¼ cups all-purpose flour
2 teaspoons baking powder
1¼ teaspoons ground cinnamon
1 teaspoon ground ginger
½ teaspoon salt
½ teaspoon ground nutmeg
⅛ teaspoon ground cloves
1 cup packed brown sugar
½ cup (1 stick) butter, softened
2 eggs
1½ teaspoons vanilla
¾ cup milk, at room temperature

Filling
2½ cups powdered sugar
¾ cup (1½ sticks) butter, softened
¼ cup canned solid-pack pumpkin
1 teaspoon ground cinnamon
½ teaspoon ground nutmeg
⅛ teaspoon ground allspice

1. For cookies, preheat oven to 350°F. Line two cookie sheets with parchment paper. Sift flour, baking powder, 1¼ teaspoons cinnamon, ginger, salt, ½ teaspoon nutmeg and cloves into medium bowl.

2. Beat brown sugar and ½ cup butter in large bowl with electric mixer at medium speed 5 minutes or until light and fluffy. Add eggs, one at a time, beating well after each addition. Beat in vanilla. Add flour mixture; beat at low speed until blended. Beat in milk until smooth. Drop rounded tablespoonfuls of batter 2 inches apart onto prepared cookie sheets.

3. Bake 10 to 12 minutes or until cookies spring back when lightly touched. Cool 2 minutes on cookie sheets. Remove to wire racks; cool completely.

4. For filling, beat powdered sugar and ¾ cup butter in large bowl with electric mixer at medium speed 3 minutes or until light and fluffy. Add pumpkin, 1 teaspoon cinnamon, ½ teaspoon nutmeg and allspice; beat until blended.

5. Spread 2 tablespoons filling on flat side of half of cookies; top with remaining cookies.   *Makes 20 whoopie pies*

TABLE OF *Contents*

CRITTER
Pops

Fun Frogs

½ baked and cooled 13×9-inch cake*
½ cup plus 2 tablespoons frosting
1 package (14 to 16 ounces) green candy coating
24 lollipop sticks
    Foam block
48 white fruit-flavored pastel candy wafers
    Chocolate sprinkles
24 (1¼-inch) pieces black string licorice
    Black decorator frosting

Prepare a cake from a mix according to package directions or use your favorite recipe. Cake must be cooled completely.

1. Line large baking sheet with waxed paper. Crumble cake into large bowl. (You should end up with fine crumbs and no large cake pieces remaining.)

2. Add frosting to cake crumbs; mix with hands until well blended. Shape mixture into 1½-inch balls (about 2 tablespoons cake mixture per ball); place on prepared baking sheet. Cover with plastic wrap; refrigerate at least 1 hour or freeze 10 minutes to firm.

3. When cake balls are firm, place candy coating in deep microwavable bowl. Melt according to package directions. Dip one lollipop stick about ½ inch into melted coating; insert stick into cake ball (no more than halfway through). Return cake pop to baking sheet in refrigerator to set. Repeat with remaining cake balls and sticks.

4. Working with one cake pop at a time, hold stick and dip cake ball into melted coating to cover completely, letting excess coating drip off. Rotate stick gently and/or tap stick on edge of bowl, if necessary, to remove excess coating. Place cake pop in foam block. Immediately attach two candy wafers to top of pop for eyes while coating is still wet; hold in place until coating is set.

5. Dip toothpick in candy coating; place two dots of coating on cake pops to attach sprinkles for nose. Apply coating to one side of each licorice piece; press onto cake pops for smile. Pipe dot of black frosting in each eye.

Makes about 24 pops

Funky Monkeys

½ baked and cooled 13×9-inch cake*
½ cup plus 2 tablespoons frosting
24 small chewy chocolate candies
 1 package (14 to 16 ounces) chocolate candy coating
24 lollipop sticks
   Foam block
48 brown candy-coated chocolate pieces
24 round yellow candies
   Black and yellow decorator frosting

Prepare a cake from a mix according to package directions or use your favorite recipe. Cake must be cooled completely.

1. Line large baking sheet with waxed paper. Crumble cake into large bowl. (You should end up with fine crumbs and no large cake pieces remaining.)

2. Add frosting to cake crumbs; mix with hands until well blended. Shape mixture into 1½-inch balls (about 2 tablespoons cake mixture per ball); place on prepared baking sheet. Cover with plastic wrap; refrigerate at least 1 hour or freeze 10 minutes to firm.

3. Meanwhile, prepare hair. Press and flatten chocolate candies into thin rectangles. (If candies are too stiff to flatten, microwave several seconds to soften.) Use scissors to make ¼-inch-long cuts across bottom (long) edge of candy. Fold candy into thirds or roll up candy so fringe is on top; separate and bend fringe pieces to create hair.

4. When cake balls are firm, place candy coating in deep microwavable bowl. Melt according to package directions. Dip one lollipop stick about ½ inch into melted coating; insert stick into cake ball (no more than halfway through). Return cake pop to baking sheet in refrigerator to set. Repeat with remaining cake balls and sticks.

5. Working with one cake pop at a time, hold stick and dip cake ball into melted coating to cover completely, letting excess coating drip off. Rotate stick gently and/or tap stick on edge of bowl, if necessary, to remove excess coating. Place cake pop in foam block. Immediately attach two chocolate pieces to sides of pop for ears while coating is still wet; hold in place until coating is set.

6. Dip toothpick in candy coating; place dot of coating in center of cake pop to attach yellow candy. Pipe two dots of black frosting above yellow candy for eyes; pipe smile on yellow candy. Pipe dot of yellow frosting in each ear. Dip toothpick in candy coating; place dot of coating on top of cake pops to attach hair. Hold in place until coating is set.   *Makes about 24 pops*

Tweet Treats

½ baked and cooled 13×9-inch cake*
½ cup plus 2 tablespoons frosting
   Yellow and orange chewy fruit candy squares or taffy strips
 1 package (14 to 16 ounces) yellow candy coating
24 lollipop sticks
   Foam block
   Black decorator frosting

Prepare a cake from a mix according to package directions or use your favorite recipe. Cake must be cooled completely.

1. Line large baking sheet with waxed paper. Crumble cake into large bowl. (You should end up with fine crumbs and no large cake pieces remaining.)

2. Add frosting to cake crumbs; mix with hands until well blended. Shape mixture into 1½-inch balls (about 2 tablespoons cake mixture per ball); place on prepared baking sheet. Cover with plastic wrap; refrigerate at least 1 hour or freeze 10 minutes to firm.

3. Meanwhile, prepare decorations. Working with one at a time, unwrap yellow candy squares and microwave on LOW (30%) 5 to 8 seconds or until softened. Press candies between hands or on waxed paper to flatten to ⅛-inch thickness. Use scissors or paring knife to cut out triangles for wings and top feathers. Repeat procedure with orange candy squares, pressing candies thinner (1⁄16 inch) and cutting into smaller triangles for beaks.

4. When cake balls are firm, place candy coating in deep microwavable bowl. Melt according to package directions. Dip one lollipop stick about ½ inch into melted coating; insert stick into cake ball (no more than halfway through). Return cake pop to baking sheet in refrigerator to set. Repeat with remaining cake balls and sticks.

5. Working with one cake pop at a time, hold stick and dip cake ball into melted coating to cover completely, letting excess coating drip off. Rotate stick gently and/or tap stick on edge of bowl, if necessary, to remove excess coating. Place cake pop in foam block. Immediately attach two yellow triangles to sides of pop for wings while coating is still wet; hold in place until coating is set.

6. Dip toothpick in candy coating; place dot of coating on top of cake pops to attach top feathers. Add dots of coating and two orange triangles for beak. Pipe two dots of black frosting above beak for eyes.

Makes about 24 pops

Nice Mice

½ baked and cooled 13×9-inch cake*
½ cup plus 2 tablespoons frosting
1 package (14 to 16 ounces) chocolate candy coating
24 lollipop sticks
Foam block
48 additional chocolate candy coating discs**
48 white round candies
24 small pink candies, mini candy-coated chocolate pieces or decors
Black decorator frosting

Prepare a cake from a mix according to package directions or use your favorite recipe. Cake must be cooled completely.
**Large chocolate nonpareil candies can also be used.*

1. Line large baking sheet with waxed paper. Crumble cake into large bowl. (You should end up with fine crumbs and no large cake pieces remaining.)

2. Add frosting to cake crumbs; mix with hands until well blended. Shape mixture into 1½-inch balls (about 2 tablespoons cake mixture per ball); place on prepared baking sheet. Cover with plastic wrap; refrigerate at least 1 hour or freeze 10 minutes to firm.

3. When cake balls are firm, place candy coating in deep microwavable bowl. Melt according to package directions. Dip one lollipop stick about ½ inch into melted coating; insert stick into cake ball (no more than halfway through). Return cake pop to baking sheet in refrigerator to set. Repeat with remaining cake balls and sticks.

4. Working with one cake pop at a time, hold stick and dip cake ball into melted coating to cover completely, letting excess coating drip off. Rotate stick gently and/or tap stick on edge of bowl, if necessary, to remove excess coating. Place cake pop in foam block. Immediately attach two chocolate discs to top of pop for ears while coating is still wet; hold in place until coating is set.

5. Dip toothpick in candy coating; place two dots of coating on cake pops to attach white candies for eyes. Add dot of coating and pink candy for nose. Pipe dot of black frosting in each eye.   *Makes about 24 pops*

Tip: To add tails, roll small pieces of chewy chocolate candies between your hands into very thin ropes. Attach to mice using melted candy coating.

Pink Pig Pops

½ baked and cooled 13×9-inch cake*
½ cup plus 2 tablespoons frosting
   Pink chewy fruit candy squares
1 package (14 to 16 ounces) pink candy coating
24 lollipop sticks
   Foam block
48 mini semisweet chocolate chips
24 pink fruit-flavored pastel candy wafers
   Black decorator frosting

Prepare a cake from a mix according to package directions or use your favorite recipe. Cake must be cooled completely.

1. Line large baking sheet with waxed paper. Crumble cake into large bowl. (You should end up with fine crumbs and no large cake pieces remaining.)

2. Add frosting to cake crumbs; mix with hands until well blended. Shape mixture into 1½-inch balls (about 2 tablespoons cake mixture per ball); place on prepared baking sheet. Cover with plastic wrap; refrigerate at least 1 hour or freeze 10 minutes to firm.

3. Meanwhile, prepare ears. Working with one at a time, unwrap candy squares and microwave on LOW (30%) 5 to 8 seconds or until softened. Press candies between hands or on waxed paper to flatten to ⅛-inch thickness. Use scissors or paring knife to cut out triangles for ears. Bend tips of ears, if desired.

4. When cake balls are firm, place candy coating in deep microwavable bowl. Melt according to package directions. Dip one lollipop stick about ½ inch into melted coating; insert stick into cake ball (no more than halfway through). Return cake pop to baking sheet in refrigerator to set. Repeat with remaining cake balls and sticks.

5. Working with one cake pop at a time, hold stick and dip cake ball into melted coating to cover completely, letting excess coating drip off. Rotate stick gently and/or tap stick on edge of bowl, if necessary, to remove excess coating. Place cake pop in foam block. Immediately attach two candy ears to top of pop while coating is still wet; hold in place until coating is set.

6. Dip toothpick in candy coating; place two dots of coating on cake pops to attach mini chips for eyes. (Cut off pointed tips of chips with knife so chips will lay flat.) Add dot of coating and candy wafer for nose. Pipe two dots of black frosting on each nose.   *Makes about 24 pops*

Tip: To add tails, roll small pieces of softened candy squares between your hands into thin ropes. Curl tails; attach to pigs using melted candy coating.

Teddy Bear Pops

½ baked and cooled 13×9-inch cake*
½ cup plus 2 tablespoons frosting
1 package (14 to 16 ounces) peanut butter candy coating
24 lollipop sticks
Foam block
1½ cups extra-large semisweet chocolate chips, divided
48 white chocolate chips
24 mini semisweet chocolate chips

Prepare a cake from a mix according to package directions or use your favorite recipe. Cake must be cooled completely.

1. Line large baking sheet with waxed paper. Crumble cake into large bowl. (You should end up with fine crumbs and no large cake pieces remaining.)

2. Add frosting to cake crumbs; mix with hands until well blended. Shape mixture into 1½-inch balls (about 2 tablespoons cake mixture per ball); place on prepared baking sheet. Cover with plastic wrap; refrigerate at least 1 hour or freeze 10 minutes to firm.

3. When cake balls are firm, place candy coating in deep microwavable bowl. Melt according to package directions. Dip one lollipop stick about ½ inch into melted coating; insert stick into cake ball (no more than halfway through). Return cake pop to baking sheet in refrigerator to set. Repeat with remaining cake balls and sticks.

4. Working with one cake pop at a time, hold stick and dip cake ball into melted coating to cover completely, letting excess coating drip off. Rotate stick gently and/or tap stick on edge of bowl, if necessary, to remove excess coating. Place cake pop in foam block. Immediately attach two large chocolate chips to top of pop for ears while coating is still wet; hold in place until coating is set.

5. Dip toothpick in candy coating; place two dots of coating on cake pops to attach white chips for eyes. Add dot of coating and mini chocolate chip for nose.

6. When all pops have ears, eyes and noses, place remaining large chocolate chips in small resealable food storage bag. Microwave on MEDIUM (50%) 45 seconds. Knead bag; microwave 30 seconds to 1 minute or until chocolate is melted and smooth. Cut off small corner of bag; pipe mouths and pupils on bear faces. *Makes about 24 pops*

Playtime *Pops*

Tiny Taffy Apples

½ baked and cooled 13×9-inch cake*
½ cup plus 2 tablespoons frosting
1 package (14 to 16 ounces) peanut butter candy coating
24 lollipop sticks
2 cups chopped peanuts
24 paper baking cups (optional)

*Prepare a cake from a mix according to package directions or use your favorite recipe.
Cake must be cooled completely.*

1. Line large baking sheet with waxed paper. Crumble cake into large bowl. (You should end up with fine crumbs and no large cake pieces remaining.)

2. Add frosting to cake crumbs; mix with hands until well blended. Shape mixture into 1½-inch balls (about 2 tablespoons cake mixture per ball); place on prepared baking sheet. Cover with plastic wrap; refrigerate at least 1 hour or freeze 10 minutes to firm.

3. When cake balls are firm, place candy coating in deep microwavable bowl. Melt according to package directions. Dip one lollipop stick about ½ inch into melted coating; insert stick into cake ball (no more than halfway through). Return cake pop to baking sheet in refrigerator to set. Repeat with remaining cake balls and sticks.

4. Place peanuts in shallow bowl. Working with one cake pop at a time, hold stick and dip cake ball into melted coating to cover completely, letting excess coating drip off. Rotate stick gently and/or tap stick on edge of bowl, if necessary, to remove excess coating.

5. Immediately roll cake pop in peanuts to coat; press in gently to adhere to coating. Place cake pops in baking cups, if desired.   *Makes about 24 pops*

High-Flying Kites

½ baked and cooled 13×9-inch cake*
½ cup plus 2 tablespoons frosting
½ (14- to 16-ounce) package purple candy coating
½ (14- to 16-ounce) package green candy coating
24 lollipop sticks
   Foam block
   Yellow decorator frosting
   Assorted color decors and small candies
   Yellow string licorice

Prepare a cake from a mix according to package directions or use your favorite recipe. Cake must be cooled completely.

1. Line large baking sheet with waxed paper. Crumble cake into large bowl. (You should end up with fine crumbs and no large cake pieces remaining.)

2. Add frosting to cake crumbs; mix with hands until well blended. Shape mixture into 1½-inch balls (about 2 tablespoons cake mixture per ball); shape balls into diamonds. Place on prepared baking sheet. Cover with plastic wrap; refrigerate at least 1 hour or freeze 10 minutes to firm.

3. When cake balls are firm, place candy coatings in separate deep microwavable bowls. Melt according to package directions. Dip one lollipop stick about ½ inch into melted coating; insert stick into cake ball (no more than halfway through). Return cake pop to baking sheet in refrigerator to set. Repeat with remaining cake balls and sticks.

4. Working with one cake pop at a time, hold stick and dip cake ball into melted coating to cover completely, letting excess coating drip off. Rotate stick gently and/or tap stick on edge of bowl, if necessary, to remove excess coating. Place cake pop in foam block.

5. Pipe crossbars on cake pops with yellow frosting. Dip toothpick in candy coating; place dots of coating on cake pops to attach decors and candies.

6. Cut licorice into desired lengths for kite tails. Attach licorice to back of cake pops using coating; hold in place until coating is set.

Makes about 24 pops

Home Run Pops

½ baked and cooled 13×9-inch cake*
½ cup plus 2 tablespoons frosting
1 package (14 to 16 ounces) white candy coating
24 lollipop sticks
   Foam block
   Red decorator frosting

Prepare a cake from a mix according to package directions or use your favorite recipe. Cake must be cooled completely.

1. Line large baking sheet with waxed paper. Crumble cake into large bowl. (You should end up with fine crumbs and no large cake pieces remaining.)

2. Add frosting to cake crumbs; mix with hands until well blended. Shape mixture into 1½-inch balls (about 2 tablespoons cake mixture per ball); place on prepared baking sheet. Cover with plastic wrap; refrigerate at least 1 hour or freeze 10 minutes to firm.

3. When cake balls are firm, place candy coating in deep microwavable bowl. Melt according to package directions. Dip one lollipop stick about ½ inch into melted coating; insert stick into cake ball (no more than halfway through). Return cake pop to baking sheet in refrigerator to set. Repeat with remaining cake balls and sticks.

4. Working with one cake pop at a time, hold stick and dip cake ball into melted coating to cover completely, letting excess coating drip off. Rotate stick gently and/or tap stick on edge of bowl, if necessary, to remove excess coating. Place cake pop in foam block.

5. Pipe seams on cake pops with red frosting.　　　　*Makes about 24 pops*

Party Poppers

½ baked and cooled 13×9-inch cake*
½ cup plus 2 tablespoons frosting
½ (14- to 16-ounce) package blue candy coating
½ (14- to 16-ounce) package red candy coating
24 lollipop sticks
  Foam block
  Red and blue gumdrops or other round candies
  Red and blue decorator frosting
  Red, white and blue sprinkles and decors

Prepare a cake from a mix according to package directions or use your favorite recipe. Cake must be cooled completely.

1. Line large baking sheet with waxed paper. Crumble cake into large bowl. (You should end up with fine crumbs and no large cake pieces remaining.)

2. Add frosting to cake crumbs; mix with hands until well blended. Shape mixture into 2½-inch-tall triangles (about 2 tablespoons cake mixture per triangle); place on prepared baking sheet. Cover with plastic wrap; refrigerate at least 1 hour or freeze 10 minutes to firm.

3. When cake balls are firm, place candy coatings in separate deep microwavable bowls. Melt according to package directions. Dip one lollipop stick about ½ inch into melted coating; insert stick into cake ball (no more than halfway through). Return cake pop to baking sheet in refrigerator to set. Repeat with remaining cake balls and sticks.

4. Working with one cake pop at a time, hold stick and dip cake ball into melted coating to cover completely, letting excess coating drip off. Rotate stick gently and/or tap stick on edge of bowl, if necessary, to remove excess coating. Place cake pop in foam block. Immediately attach gumdrop to top of pop while coating is still wet; hold in place until coating is set. (Or omit gumdrop and pipe decorator frosting on top of cake pop instead.)

5. Pipe decorator frosting along bottom of each cake pop. Pipe dots on cake pops with frosting, or dip toothpick in candy coating and place dots of coating on cake pops to attach sprinkles and decors.   *Makes about 24 pops*

Earth Pops

½ baked and cooled 13×9-inch cake*
½ cup plus 2 tablespoons frosting
1 package (14 to 16 ounces) blue candy coating
½ (14- to 16-ounce) package green candy coating
24 lollipop sticks
   Foam block

Prepare a cake from a mix according to package directions or use your favorite recipe. Cake must be cooled completely.

1. Line large baking sheet with waxed paper. Crumble cake into large bowl. (You should end up with fine crumbs and no large cake pieces remaining.)

2. Add frosting to cake crumbs; mix with hands until well blended. Shape mixture into 1½-inch balls (about 2 tablespoons cake mixture per ball); place on prepared baking sheet. Cover with plastic wrap; refrigerate at least 1 hour or freeze 10 minutes to firm.

3. When cake balls are firm, place candy coatings in separate deep microwavable bowls. Melt according to package directions. Dip one lollipop stick about ½ inch into melted blue coating; insert stick into cake ball (no more than halfway through). Return cake pop to baking sheet in refrigerator to set. Repeat with remaining cake balls and sticks.

4. Working with one cake pop at a time, hold stick and dip cake ball into melted blue coating to cover completely, letting excess coating drip off. Rotate stick gently and/or tap stick on edge of bowl, if necessary, to remove excess coating.

5. Immediately drizzle cake pop with melted green coating using fork or spoon, turning pop constantly while drizzling. (For green swirls to set smoothly in blue coating, pop must be turned or shaken while drizzling, and drizzling must be done while blue coating is still wet.) Place cake pop in foam block to set.

Makes about 24 pops

Touchdown Treats

½ baked and cooled 13×9-inch cake*
½ cup plus 2 tablespoons frosting
1 package (14 to 16 ounces) chocolate candy coating
24 lollipop sticks
Foam block
White decorator frosting

Prepare a cake from a mix according to package directions or use your favorite recipe. Cake must be cooled completely.

1. Line large baking sheet with waxed paper. Crumble cake into large bowl. (You should end up with fine crumbs and no large cake pieces remaining.)

2. Add frosting to cake crumbs; mix with hands until well blended. Shape mixture into tapered oval footballs (about 2 tablespoons cake mixture per football); place on prepared baking sheet. Cover with plastic wrap; refrigerate at least 1 hour or freeze 10 minutes to firm.

3. When cake balls are firm, place candy coating in deep microwavable bowl. Melt according to package directions. Dip one lollipop stick about ½ inch into melted coating; insert stick into cake ball (no more than halfway through). Return cake pop to baking sheet in refrigerator to set. Repeat with remaining cake balls and sticks.

4. Working with one cake pop at a time, hold stick and dip cake ball into melted coating to cover completely, letting excess coating drip off. Rotate stick gently and/or tap stick on edge of bowl, if necessary, to remove excess coating. Place cake pop in foam block.

5. Pipe laces on cake pops with white frosting. *Makes about 24 pops*

Lucky Dice Pops

½ baked and cooled 13×9-inch cake*
½ cup plus 2 tablespoons frosting
1 package (14 to 16 ounces) white candy coating
24 lollipop sticks
   Foam block
   Black decorator frosting or black gel frosting

Prepare a cake from a mix according to package directions or use your favorite recipe. Cake must be cooled completely.

1. Line large baking sheet with waxed paper. Crumble cake into large bowl. (You should end up with fine crumbs and no large cake pieces remaining.)

2. Add frosting to cake crumbs; mix with hands until well blended. Shape mixture into 1½-inch balls (about 2 tablespoons cake mixture per ball); shape balls into squares. Place on prepared baking sheet. Cover with plastic wrap; refrigerate at least 1 hour or freeze 10 minutes to firm.

3. When cake balls are firm, place candy coating in deep microwavable bowl. Melt according to package directions. Dip one lollipop stick about ½ inch into melted coating; insert stick into cake ball (no more than halfway through). Return cake pop to baking sheet in refrigerator to set. Repeat with remaining cake balls and sticks.

4. Working with one cake pop at a time, hold stick and dip cake ball into melted coating to cover completely, letting excess coating drip off. Rotate stick gently and/or tap stick on edge of bowl, if necessary, to remove excess coating. Place cake pop in foam block.

5. Pipe dots on top and sides of cake pops with black frosting.

Makes about 24 pops

Balloon Pops

½ baked and cooled 13×9-inch cake*
½ cup plus 2 tablespoons frosting
   Red, yellow or blue chewy fruit candy squares or taffy strips
1 package (14 to 16 ounces) red, yellow or blue candy coating
24 lollipop sticks
   Foam block

Prepare a cake from a mix according to package directions or use your favorite recipe. Cake must be cooled completely.

1. Line large baking sheet with waxed paper. Crumble cake into large bowl. (You should end up with fine crumbs and no large cake pieces remaining.)

2. Add frosting to cake crumbs; mix with hands until well blended. Shape mixture into 1½-inch balls (about 2 tablespoons cake mixture per ball); place on prepared baking sheet. Cover with plastic wrap; refrigerate at least 1 hour or freeze 10 minutes to firm.

3. Meanwhile, prepare balloon knots. Unwrap candy squares; cut each into four pieces. Working with one piece at a time, microwave on LOW (30%) 5 seconds or until softened. Press candy between hands or on waxed paper to flatten and shape into ⅛-inch-thick circle. Use end of lollipop stick to poke hole in center of circle; bend circle into cone shape to resemble balloon knot.

4. When cake balls are firm, place candy coating in deep microwavable bowl. Melt according to package directions. Dip one lollipop stick about ½ inch into melted coating; insert stick into cake ball (no more than halfway through). Return cake pop to baking sheet in refrigerator to set. Repeat with remaining cake balls and sticks.

5. Working with one cake pop at a time, hold stick and dip cake ball into melted coating to cover completely, letting excess coating drip off. Rotate stick gently and/or tap stick on edge of bowl, if necessary, to remove excess coating. Place cake pop in foam block.

6. Dip toothpick in candy coating; place dots of coating around base of each cake pop where stick is attached. Slide candy balloon knot up stick and attach to base of cake pop; hold in place until coating is set.

Makes about 24 pops

Spicy Chocolate Pops

½ baked and cooled 13×9-inch chocolate cake* (see Tip)
½ cup plus 2 tablespoons chocolate frosting
1 package (14 to 16 ounces) chocolate candy coating
24 lollipop sticks
   Ground red pepper
   Ground cinnamon
   Foam block

*Prepare a cake from a mix according to package directions or use your favorite recipe.
Cake must be cooled completely.*

1. Line large baking sheet with waxed paper. Crumble cake into large bowl.
(You should end up with fine crumbs and no large cake pieces remaining.)

2. Add frosting to cake crumbs; mix with hands until well blended. Shape
mixture into 1½-inch balls (about 2 tablespoons cake mixture per ball); place
on prepared baking sheet. Cover with plastic wrap; refrigerate at least 1 hour
or freeze 10 minutes to firm.

3. When cake balls are firm, place candy coating in deep microwavable bowl.
Melt according to package directions. Dip one lollipop stick about ½ inch into
melted coating; insert stick into cake ball (no more than halfway through).
Return cake pop to baking sheet in refrigerator to set. Repeat with remaining
cake balls and sticks.

4. Working with one cake pop at a time, hold stick and dip cake ball into
melted coating to cover completely, letting excess coating drip off. Rotate
stick gently and/or tap stick on edge of bowl, if necessary, to remove excess
coating.

5. Immediately sprinkle cake pop lightly with red pepper and cinnamon while
coating is still wet. Place cake pop in foam block to set.

Makes about 24 pops

TIP   For a spicier chocolate flavor, add 1 teaspoon ground
cinnamon and ¼ to ½ teaspoon ground red pepper to the
batter when preparing your chocolate cake.

Pretty Package Pops

½ baked and cooled 13×9-inch cake*
½ cup plus 2 tablespoons frosting
½ (14- to 16-ounce) package blue candy coating
½ (14- to 16-ounce) package purple candy coating
24 lollipop sticks
  Foam block
  Assorted color taffy and gummy strips
  Assorted color spice drops or gumdrops

Prepare a cake from a mix according to package directions or use your favorite recipe. Cake must be cooled completely.

1. Line large baking sheet with waxed paper. Crumble cake into large bowl. (You should end up with fine crumbs and no large cake pieces remaining.)

2. Add frosting to cake crumbs; mix with hands until well blended. Shape mixture into 1½-inch balls (about 2 tablespoons cake mixture per ball); shape balls into squares. Place on prepared baking sheet. Cover with plastic wrap; refrigerate at least 1 hour or freeze 10 minutes to firm.

3. When cake balls are firm, place candy coatings in separate deep microwavable bowls. Melt according to package directions. Dip one lollipop stick about ½ inch into melted coating; insert stick into cake ball (no more than halfway through). Return cake pop to baking sheet in refrigerator to set. Repeat with remaining cake balls and sticks.

4. Working with one cake pop at a time, hold stick and dip cake ball into melted coating to cover completely, letting excess coating drip off. Rotate stick gently and/or tap stick on edge of bowl, if necessary, to remove excess coating. Place cake pop in foam block.

5. Cut pieces of taffy or gummy strips with scissors to fit around cake pops for ribbons. Apply coating to back of each taffy piece with toothpick; press onto cake pops and hold until coating is set.

6. For candy bows, cut slits in top of spice drops (cut about halfway through candies). Separate cut pieces of spice drops, pressing them outward to resemble loops of bow. (For bigger bow, cut small pieces from additional spice drop and press them into center of bow.) Dip toothpick in candy coating; place dot of coating on top of cake pops to attach bows.   *Makes about 24 pops*

Tip: Instead of using taffy and spice drops, you can pipe decorator frosting around and on top of the cake pops to create ribbons and bows.

Holiday
Pops

Sweetheart Pops

½ baked and cooled 13×9-inch cake*
½ cup plus 2 tablespoons frosting
1 package (14 to 16 ounces) pink candy coating
24 lollipop sticks
    Foam block
    White decors, sugar pearls or sprinkles

Prepare a cake from a mix according to package directions or use your favorite recipe. Cake must be cooled completely.

1. Line large baking sheet with waxed paper. Crumble cake into large bowl. (You should end up with fine crumbs and no large cake pieces remaining.)

2. Add frosting to cake crumbs; mix with hands until well blended. Shape mixture into 1½-inch balls (about 2 tablespoons cake mixture per ball); shape balls into hearts. Place on prepared baking sheet. Cover with plastic wrap; refrigerate at least 1 hour or freeze 10 minutes to firm.

3. When cake balls are firm, place candy coating in deep microwavable bowl. Melt according to package directions. Dip one lollipop stick about ½ inch into melted coating; insert stick into cake ball (no more than halfway through). Return cake pop to baking sheet in refrigerator to set. Repeat with remaining cake balls and sticks.

4. Working with one cake pop at a time, hold stick and dip cake ball into melted coating to cover completely, letting excess coating drip off. Rotate stick gently and/or tap stick on edge of bowl, if necessary, to remove excess coating. Place cake pop in foam block.

5. Dip toothpick in candy coating; place dots of coating on cake pops to attach decors and sugar pearls.   *Makes about 24 pops*

Variation: For quicker decorating, use white decorator frosting instead of decors. Pipe dots, hearts or stripes on cake pops as desired.

Sweet Swirly Pops

½ baked and cooled 13×9-inch cake*
½ cup plus 2 tablespoons frosting
½ (14- to 16-ounce) package chocolate candy coating
½ (14- to 16-ounce) package white candy coating
½ (14- to 16-ounce) package pink and/or red candy coating
24 lollipop sticks
    Foam block

Prepare a cake from a mix according to package directions or use your favorite recipe. Cake must be cooled completely.

1. Line large baking sheet with waxed paper. Crumble cake into large bowl. (You should end up with fine crumbs and no large cake pieces remaining.)

2. Add frosting to cake crumbs; mix with hands until well blended. Shape mixture into 1½-inch balls (about 2 tablespoons cake mixture per ball); place on prepared baking sheet. Cover with plastic wrap; refrigerate at least 1 hour or freeze 10 minutes to firm.

3. When cake balls are firm, place candy coatings in separate deep microwavable bowls. Melt according to package directions. Dip one lollipop stick about ½ inch into melted coating; insert stick into cake ball (no more than halfway through). Return cake pop to baking sheet in refrigerator to set. Repeat with remaining cake balls and sticks.

4. Working with one cake pop at a time, hold stick and dip cake ball into melted chocolate or white coating to cover completely, letting excess coating drip off. Rotate stick gently and/or tap stick on edge of bowl, if necessary, to remove excess coating.

5. Immediately drizzle cake pop with melted pink or red coating using fork or spoon, turning pop constantly while drizzling. (For swirls to set smoothly in base coating, pop must be turned or shaken while drizzling, and drizzling must be done while base coating is still wet.) Place cake pop in foam block to set.

Makes about 24 pops

Tip: To make cake pops with two color swirls, drizzle cake pop with both colors immediately after dipping in base coating as directed in step 5.

Easter Egg Pops

½ baked and cooled 13×9-inch cake*
½ cup plus 2 tablespoons frosting
½ (14- to 16-ounce) package pink candy coating
½ (14- to 16-ounce) package yellow candy coating
24 lollipop sticks
   Foam block
   White, yellow and pink decorator frosting
   Pastel-colored decors or sugar pearls

Prepare a cake from a mix according to package directions or use your favorite recipe. Cake must be cooled completely.

1. Line large baking sheet with waxed paper. Crumble cake into large bowl. (You should end up with fine crumbs and no large cake pieces remaining.)

2. Add frosting to cake crumbs; mix with hands until well blended. Shape mixture into 1½-inch eggs (about 2 tablespoons cake mixture per egg); place on prepared baking sheet. Cover with plastic wrap; refrigerate at least 1 hour or freeze 10 minutes to firm.

3. When cake balls are firm, place candy coatings in separate deep microwavable bowls. Melt according to package directions. Dip one lollipop stick about ½ inch into melted coating; insert stick into cake ball (no more than halfway through). Return cake pop to baking sheet in refrigerator to set. Repeat with remaining cake balls and sticks.

4. Working with one cake pop at a time, hold stick and dip cake ball into melted coating to cover completely, letting excess coating drip off. Rotate stick gently and/or tap stick on edge of bowl, if necessary, to remove excess coating. Place cake pop in foam block.

5. Pipe designs on cake pops with decorator frosting. Dip toothpick in candy coating; place dots of coating on cake pops to attach decors and sugar pearls.

Makes about 24 pops

Hoppin' Pops

½ baked and cooled 13×9-inch cake*
½ cup plus 2 tablespoons frosting
½ (14- to 16-ounce) package yellow candy coating
½ (14- to 16-ounce) package pink candy coating
24 lollipop sticks
   Foam block
   Mini semisweet chocolate chips
   White decorator frosting
   Granulated sugar

Prepare a cake from a mix according to package directions or use your favorite recipe. Cake must be cooled completely.

1. Line large baking sheet with waxed paper. Crumble cake into large bowl. (You should end up with fine crumbs and no large cake pieces remaining.)

2. Add frosting to cake crumbs; mix with hands until well blended. Shape mixture into bunny heads (about 2 tablespoons cake mixture per head); place on prepared baking sheet. Cover with plastic wrap; refrigerate at least 1 hour or freeze 10 minutes to firm.

3. When cake balls are firm, place candy coatings in separate deep microwavable bowls. Melt according to package directions. Dip one lollipop stick about ½ inch into melted coating; insert stick into cake ball (no more than halfway through). Return cake pop to baking sheet in refrigerator to set. Repeat with remaining cake balls and sticks.

4. Working with one cake pop at a time, hold stick and dip cake ball into melted coating to cover completely, letting excess coating drip off. Rotate stick gently and/or tap stick on edge of bowl, if necessary, to remove excess coating. Place cake pop in foam block. Immediately attach two mini chips to pop for eyes while coating is still wet; hold in place until coating is set.

5. Dip toothpick in candy coating; place dot of coating below eyes to attach additional mini chip for nose.

6. Pipe white frosting in center of each ear; sprinkle with sugar to coat. Brush off any excess sugar from cake pops.   *Makes about 24 pops*

Easy Easter Pops

½ baked and cooled 13×9-inch cake*
½ cup plus 2 tablespoons frosting
½ (14- to 16-ounce) package yellow candy coating
½ (14- to 16-ounce) package purple candy coating
24 lollipop sticks
   Foam block

Prepare a cake from a mix according to package directions or use your favorite recipe. Cake must be cooled completely.

1. Line large baking sheet with waxed paper. Crumble cake into large bowl. (You should end up with fine crumbs and no large cake pieces remaining.)

2. Add frosting to cake crumbs; mix with hands until well blended. Shape mixture into 1½-inch balls (about 2 tablespoons cake mixture per ball); place on prepared baking sheet. Cover with plastic wrap; refrigerate at least 1 hour or freeze 10 minutes to firm.

3. When cake balls are firm, place candy coatings in separate deep microwavable bowls. Melt according to package directions. Dip one lollipop stick about ½ inch into melted coating; insert stick into cake ball (no more than halfway through). Return cake pop to baking sheet in refrigerator to set. Repeat with remaining cake balls and sticks.

4. Working with one cake pop at a time, hold stick and dip cake ball into melted coating to cover completely, letting excess coating drip off. Rotate stick gently and/or tap stick on edge of bowl, if necessary, to remove excess coating. Place cake pop in foam block to set.

5. Transfer remaining candy coatings to two small resealable food storage bags. (Reheat briefly in microwave if coatings have hardened.) Cut off small corner of each bag; drizzle pops with contrasting color coating.

Makes about 24 pops

Pumpkin Patch Pops

½ baked and cooled 13×9-inch cake*
½ cup plus 2 tablespoons frosting
1½ packages (14 to 16 ounces each) orange candy coating
24 lollipop sticks
　Green gumdrops or spice drops
　Foam block

Prepare a cake from a mix according to package directions or use your favorite recipe. Cake must be cooled completely.

1. Line large baking sheet with waxed paper. Crumble cake into large bowl. (You should end up with fine crumbs and no large cake pieces remaining.)

2. Add frosting to cake crumbs; mix with hands until well blended. Shape mixture into 1½-inch balls (about 2 tablespoons cake mixture per ball); make indentation in top of each ball for stem. Place on prepared baking sheet. Cover with plastic wrap; refrigerate at least 1 hour or freeze 10 minutes to firm.

3. When cake balls are firm, place candy coating in deep microwavable bowl. Melt according to package directions. Dip one lollipop stick about ½ inch into melted coating; insert stick into cake ball (no more than halfway through). Return cake pop to baking sheet in refrigerator to set. Repeat with remaining cake balls and sticks.

4. Cut gumdrops in half, if necessary, to create stems. Working with one cake pop at a time, hold stick and dip cake ball into melted coating to cover completely, letting excess coating drip off. Rotate stick gently and/or tap stick on edge of bowl, if necessary, to remove excess coating. Place cake pop in foam block. Immediately attach gumdrop to top of pop while coating is still wet; hold in place until coating is set.

5. Transfer remaining candy coating to small resealable food storage bag. (Reheat briefly in microwave if coating has hardened.) Cut off small corner of bag; pipe vertical lines on each cake pop from stem to stick. Pipe coating around stem, if desired.　　　　　　　　　　　　　*Makes about 24 pops*

Variation: You can use orange decorator frosting instead of the candy coating to pipe the lines on the cake pops.

Boo Bites

  ½ baked and cooled 13×9-inch cake*
  ½ cup plus 2 tablespoons frosting
  1 package (14 to 16 ounces) white candy coating
 24 lollipop sticks
    Foam block
    Black decorator frosting or black gel frosting

Prepare a cake from a mix according to package directions or use your favorite recipe. Cake must be cooled completely.

1. Line large baking sheet with waxed paper. Crumble cake into large bowl. (You should end up with fine crumbs and no large cake pieces remaining.)

2. Add frosting to cake crumbs; mix with hands until well blended. Shape mixture into 2-inch-tall rounded triangles (about 2 tablespoons cake mixture per triangle). Place on prepared baking sheet. Cover with plastic wrap; refrigerate at least 1 hour or freeze 10 minutes to firm.

3. When cake balls are firm, place candy coating in deep microwavable bowl. Melt according to package directions. Dip one lollipop stick about ½ inch into melted coating; insert stick into cake ball (no more than halfway through). Return cake pop to baking sheet in refrigerator to set. Repeat with remaining cake balls and sticks.

4. Working with one cake pop at a time, hold stick and dip cake ball into melted coating to cover completely, letting excess coating drip off. Rotate stick gently and/or tap stick on edge of bowl, if necessary, to remove excess coating. Place cake pop in foam block.

5. Pipe eyes and mouths on cake pops with black frosting.

Makes about 24 pops

Freaky Frank

½ baked and cooled 13×9-inch cake*
½ cup plus 2 tablespoons frosting
  Small chewy chocolate candies
  Green taffy candies
1 package (14 to 16 ounces) green candy coating
24 lollipop sticks
  Foam block
  Black and white decorator frosting

Prepare a cake from a mix according to package directions or use your favorite recipe. Cake must be cooled completely.

1. Line large baking sheet with waxed paper. Crumble cake into large bowl. (You should end up with fine crumbs and no large cake pieces remaining.)

2. Add frosting to cake crumbs; mix with hands until well blended. Shape mixture into 1½-inch balls (about 2 tablespoons cake mixture per ball); shape balls into squares with rounded bottoms. Place on prepared baking sheet. Cover with plastic wrap; refrigerate at least 1 hour or freeze 10 minutes to firm.

3. Meanwhile, prepare decorations. Cut two small pieces from chocolate candy; roll into bolts. Press remaining piece into rectangle for hair. Working with one piece at a time, unwrap taffy and microwave on LOW (30%) 5 to 10 seconds or until softened. Cut small strip from taffy; flatten into rectangle for forehead. Cut three small pieces; shape into ears and nose.

4. When cake balls are firm, place candy coating in deep microwavable bowl. Melt according to package directions. Dip one lollipop stick about ½ inch into melted coating; insert stick into cake ball (no more than halfway through). Return to baking sheet in refrigerator to set. Repeat with remaining cake balls and sticks.

5. Working with one cake pop at a time, hold stick and dip cake ball into melted coating to cover completely, letting excess coating drip off. Rotate stick gently and/or tap stick on edge of bowl, if necessary, to remove excess coating. Place cake pop in foam block. Immediately attach hair and forehead while coating is still wet; hold in place until coating is set.

6. Dip toothpick in candy coating; place dots of coating on cake pops to attach ears, nose and bolts. Pipe black frosting over chocolate candy for hair. Pipe eyes and squiggle for mouth. Pipe dot of white frosting in each eye.

7. Transfer remaining candy coating to small resealable food storage bag. (Reheat briefly in microwave if coating has hardened.) Cut off small corner of bag; pipe stitches along one side of face.   *Makes about 24 pops*

Cutie Corn

½ baked and cooled 13×9-inch cake*
½ cup plus 2 tablespoons frosting
   Yellow and orange chewy fruit candy squares
 1 package (14 to 16 ounces) orange candy coating
 1 package (14 to 16 ounces) yellow candy coating
 ½ (14- to 16-ounce) package white candy coating
24 lollipop sticks
   Foam block
   Black decorator frosting

Prepare a cake from a mix according to package directions or use your favorite recipe. Cake must be cooled completely.

1. Line large baking sheet with waxed paper. Crumble cake into large bowl. (You should end up with fine crumbs and no large cake pieces remaining.)

2. Add frosting to cake crumbs; mix with hands until well blended. Shape mixture into 1½-inch balls (about 2 tablespoons cake mixture per ball); shape balls into triangles. Place on prepared baking sheet. Cover with plastic wrap; refrigerate at least 1 hour or freeze 10 minutes to firm.

3. Meanwhile, prepare decorations. Working with one at a time, unwrap candy and microwave on LOW (30%) 5 to 10 seconds or until softened. Cut two small pieces from yellow candy; roll into balls for eyes. Cut small piece from orange candy; roll into teardrop shape for nose.

4. When cake balls are firm, place yellow candy coating in deep microwavable bowl. Melt according to package directions. Dip one lollipop stick about ½ inch into melted coating; insert stick into cake ball (no more than halfway through). Return to baking sheet in refrigerator to set. Repeat with remaining cake balls and sticks.

5. Working with one cake pop at a time, hold stick and dip cake ball into melted yellow coating to cover completely, letting excess coating drip off. Rotate stick gently and/or tap stick on edge of bowl, if necessary, to remove excess coating. Place cake pop in foam block; let stand until set.

6. Melt orange candy coating; dip all but one third of cake pop into coating. Place in foam block; let stand until set. Melt white candy coating; dip top third of cake pop into coating. Place cake pop in foam block. Immediately attach eyes and nose while coating is still wet; hold in place until coating is set.

7. Pipe mouth and dot in each eye with black frosting.

Makes about 24 pops

Silly Skeleton

½ baked and cooled 13×9-inch cake*
½ cup plus 2 tablespoons frosting
   Green and yellow taffy candies
   Orange chewy fruit candy squares
1 package (14 to 16 ounces) white candy coating
24 lollipop sticks
   Foam block
   Black decorator frosting

Prepare a cake from a mix according to package directions or use your favorite recipe. Cake must be cooled completely.

1. Line large baking sheet with waxed paper. Crumble cake into large bowl. (You should end up with fine crumbs and no large cake pieces remaining.)

2. Add frosting to cake crumbs; mix with hands until well blended. Shape mixture into 1½-inch balls (about 2 tablespoons cake mixture per ball); shape balls into ovals. Place on prepared baking sheet. Cover with plastic wrap; refrigerate at least 1 hour or freeze 10 minutes to firm.

3. Meanwhile, prepare decorations. Working with one at a time, unwrap taffy candy and microwave on LOW (30%) 5 to 10 seconds or until softened. Flatten green candy; use scissors or paring knife to cut out small rectangles for eyes. Cut two small pieces from yellow candy; roll into balls for eyes. Unwrap orange candy square and microwave on LOW (30%) 5 to 10 seconds or until softened. Cut two small pieces; roll into smaller balls for eyes. Cut tiny pieces for teeth.

4. When cake balls are firm, place candy coating in deep microwavable bowl. Melt according to package directions. Dip one lollipop stick about ½ inch into melted coating; insert stick into cake ball (no more than halfway through). Return to baking sheet in refrigerator to set. Repeat with remaining cake balls and sticks.

5. Working with one cake pop at a time, hold stick and dip cake ball into melted coating to cover completely, letting excess coating drip off. Rotate stick gently and/or tap stick on edge of bowl, if necessary, to remove excess coating. Place cake pop in foam block. Immediately attach green taffy pieces for eyes while coating is still wet; hold in place until coating is set.

6. Dip toothpick in candy coating; place dots of coating on green taffy to attach orange and yellow balls to eyes. Pipe long teardrop shape for nose and line for mouth with black frosting. Use candy coating to attach teeth just below mouth.   *Makes about 24 pops*

Wicked Witch

½ baked and cooled 13×9-inch cake*
½ cup plus 2 tablespoons frosting
   Green, purple and yellow taffy candies
 1 package (14 to 16 ounces) green candy coating
24 lollipop sticks
   Foam block
24 milk chocolate kiss candies
24 chocolate wafer cookies
   Black decorator frosting

Prepare a cake from a mix according to package directions or use your favorite recipe. Cake must be cooled completely.

1. Line large baking sheet with waxed paper. Crumble cake into large bowl. (You should end up with fine crumbs and no large cake pieces remaining.)

2. Add frosting to cake crumbs; mix with hands until well blended. Shape mixture into 1½-inch balls (about 2 tablespoons cake mixture per ball); shape into rounded triangles. Place on prepared baking sheet. Cover with plastic wrap; refrigerate at least 1 hour or freeze 10 minutes to firm.

3. Meanwhile, prepare decorations. Working with one at a time, unwrap taffy candy and microwave on LOW (30%) 5 to 10 seconds or until softened. Flatten green and purple taffy candies. Use scissors or paring knife to cut small triangles from green candy for noses. Roll small pieces of green candy into balls for warts. Cut and roll strips of purple candy for hair. Cut small pieces from yellow candy; roll into balls for eyes.

4. When cake balls are firm, place candy coating in deep microwavable bowl. Melt according to package directions. Dip one lollipop stick about ½ inch into melted coating; insert stick into cake ball (no more than halfway through). Return to baking sheet in refrigerator to set. Repeat with remaining cake balls and sticks.

5. Working with one cake pop at a time, hold stick and dip cake ball into melted coating to cover completely, letting excess coating drip off. Rotate stick gently and/or tap stick on edge of bowl, if necessary, to remove excess coating. Place cake pop in foam block. Immediately attach eyes and nose while coating is still wet; hold in place until coating is set.

6. Dip toothpick in candy coating; place dots of coating on cake pop to attach wart and hair. Attach chocolate candy to center of wafer cookie using coating; attach hat to top of cake pop using coating. Pipe mouth and dot in each eye with black frosting.   *Makes about 24 pops*

Jolly Pops

½ baked and cooled 13×9-inch cake*
½ cup plus 2 tablespoons frosting
1 package (14 to 16 ounces) red candy coating
24 lollipop sticks
    Foam block
    White candies, gumdrops or mini marshmallows
    White decorator frosting

Prepare a cake from a mix according to package directions or use your favorite recipe. Cake must be cooled completely.

1. Line large baking sheet with waxed paper. Crumble cake into large bowl. (You should end up with fine crumbs and no large cake pieces remaining.)

2. Add frosting to cake crumbs; mix with hands until well blended. Shape mixture into 2½-inch-tall triangles (about 2 tablespoons cake mixture per triangle); place on prepared baking sheet. Cover with plastic wrap; refrigerate at least 1 hour or freeze 10 minutes to firm.

3. When cake balls are firm, place candy coating in deep microwavable bowl. Melt according to package directions. Dip one lollipop stick about ½ inch into melted coating; insert stick into cake ball (no more than halfway through). Return cake pop to baking sheet in refrigerator to set. Repeat with remaining cake balls and sticks.

4. Working with one cake pop at a time, hold stick and dip cake ball into melted coating to cover completely, letting excess coating drip off. Rotate stick gently and/or tap stick on edge of bowl, if necessary, to remove excess coating. Place cake pop in foam block. Immediately attach candy to top of pop while coating is still wet; hold in place until coating is set.

5. Pipe white frosting along bottom of each cake pop.

Makes about 24 pops

Ornament Pops

½ baked and cooled 13×9-inch cake*
½ cup plus 2 tablespoons frosting
1 package (14 to 16 ounces) white candy coating
24 lollipop sticks
   Foam block
   Red or yellow string licorice, cut into 1½-inch lengths
   Red and green gumdrops or gummy candies
   Assorted color candies, sprinkles, decors, sugar pearls and
      sparkling sugar
   Red, white and green decorator frosting

Prepare a cake from a mix according to package directions or use your favorite recipe. Cake must be cooled completely.

1. Line large baking sheet with waxed paper. Crumble cake into large bowl. (You should end up with fine crumbs and no large cake pieces remaining.)

2. Add frosting to cake crumbs; mix with hands until well blended. Shape mixture into 1½-inch balls (about 2 tablespoons cake mixture per ball); place on prepared baking sheet. Cover with plastic wrap; refrigerate at least 1 hour or freeze 10 minutes to firm.

3. When cake balls are firm, place candy coating in deep microwavable bowl. Melt according to package directions. Dip one lollipop stick about ½ inch into melted coating; insert stick into cake ball (no more than halfway through). Return cake pop to baking sheet in refrigerator to set. Repeat with remaining cake balls and sticks.

4. Working with one cake pop at a time, hold stick and dip cake ball into melted coating to cover completely, letting excess coating drip off. Rotate stick gently and/or tap stick on edge of bowl, if necessary, to remove excess coating. Place cake pop in foam block. Immediately push both ends of licorice piece into top of pop to form hanger while coating is still wet; hold in place until coating is set. (Or press gumdrop or other candy into top of pop.)

5. Decorate cake pops with candies, sprinkles, decors, sugar pearls and sugar, using coating to attach decorations. Pipe designs on cake pops with decorator frosting.   *Makes about 24 pops*

Reindeer Pops

½ baked and cooled 13×9-inch cake*
½ cup plus 2 tablespoons frosting
1 package (14 to 16 ounces) chocolate candy coating
24 lollipop sticks
48 small pretzel twists
   Foam block
48 semisweet chocolate chips
48 round white candies
24 red candy-coated chocolate pieces
   Black decorator frosting or black gel frosting

Prepare a cake from a mix according to package directions or use your favorite recipe. Cake must be cooled completely.

1. Line large baking sheet with waxed paper. Crumble cake into large bowl. (You should end up with fine crumbs and no large cake pieces remaining.)

2. Add frosting to cake crumbs; mix with hands until well blended. Shape mixture into rounded triangles or skull shape (about 2 tablespoons cake mixture per triangle); place on prepared baking sheet. Cover with plastic wrap; refrigerate at least 1 hour or freeze 10 minutes to firm.

3. When cake balls are firm, place candy coating in deep microwavable bowl. Melt according to package directions. Dip one lollipop stick about ½ inch into melted coating; insert stick into cake ball (no more than halfway through). Return cake pop to baking sheet in refrigerator to set. Repeat with remaining cake balls and sticks.

4. Break off one section from each pretzel twist; set aside.

5. Working with one cake pop at a time, hold stick and dip cake ball into melted coating to cover completely, letting excess coating drip off. Rotate stick gently and/or tap stick on edge of bowl, if necessary, to remove excess coating. Place cake pop in foam block. Immediately attach two pretzel twists to top of pop for antlers while coating is still wet; hold in place until coating is set.

6. Dip toothpick in candy coating; place two dots of coating on either side of pretzel twists to attach chocolate chips for ears. Add two dots of coating and white candies for eyes. Add dot of coating and chocolate piece for nose. Pipe dot of black frosting in center of each eye.   *Makes about 24 pops*

Frosty's Friends

½ baked and cooled 13×9-inch cake*
½ cup plus 2 tablespoons frosting
1 package (14 to 16 ounces) white candy coating
16 lollipop sticks
    Foam block
    Orange candy-coated chocolate pieces or sunflower seeds
    Assorted color decors and candy dots
    Black decorator frosting or black gel frosting
    Assorted color taffy, gummy strings or string licorice
    Assorted color gumdrops, candy discs and chocolate kisses

Prepare a cake from a mix according to package directions or use your favorite recipe. Cake must be cooled completely.

1. Line large baking sheet with waxed paper. Crumble cake into large bowl. (You should end up with fine crumbs and no large cake pieces remaining.)

2. Add frosting to cake crumbs; mix with hands until well blended. Shape mixture into 24 (1½-inch) balls (about 2 tablespoons cake mixture per ball); place 16 balls on prepared baking sheet. Divide each of remaining 8 balls in half; shape into smaller balls for heads and place on baking sheet. Cover with plastic wrap; refrigerate at least 1 hour or freeze 10 minutes to firm.

3. When cake balls are firm, place candy coating in deep microwavable bowl. Melt according to package directions. Dip one lollipop stick about 1 inch into melted coating; insert stick through larger cake ball so ½ inch of stick comes out top of cake ball. Dip end of stick in melted coating again; insert stick into smaller cake ball to create snowman head. (Cake balls should be touching.) Return cake pop to baking sheet in refrigerator to set. Repeat with remaining cake balls and sticks.

4. Working with one cake pop at a time, hold stick and dip cake balls into melted coating to cover completely, letting excess coating drip off. Rotate stick gently and/or tap stick on edge of bowl, if necessary, to remove excess coating. Place cake pop in foam block.

5. Cut orange candies in half for noses. Dip toothpick in candy coating; place dot of coating on cake pops to attach candy nose. Attach decors to snowman bodies for buttons. Pipe eyes and mouths with black frosting.

6. Cut or stretch taffy or gummy strings into long thin pieces for scarves. Carefully tie scarves around snowman necks. Create hats using candies, decors and licorice as shown in photo. Attach hats to snowman heads using dots of coating.   *Makes about 16 pops*

Tip: For more elaborate scarves, cut lengths of taffy or gummy strings and braid them together. Cut the edges of the candies to resemble fringe.

Christmas Tree Pops

½ baked and cooled 13×9-inch cake*
½ cup plus 2 tablespoons frosting
1 package (14 to 16 ounces) green candy coating
24 lollipop sticks
   Foam block
24 white candy stars
   Red and white decorator frosting

Prepare a cake from a mix according to package directions or use your favorite recipe. Cake must be cooled completely.

1. Line large baking sheet with waxed paper. Crumble cake into large bowl. (You should end up with fine crumbs and no large cake pieces remaining.)

2. Add frosting to cake crumbs; mix with hands until well blended. Shape mixture into 2½-inch-tall triangles (about 2 tablespoons cake mixture per triangle); place on prepared baking sheet. Cover with plastic wrap; refrigerate at least 1 hour or freeze 10 minutes to firm.

3. When cake balls are firm, place candy coating in deep microwavable bowl. Melt according to package directions. Dip one lollipop stick about ½ inch into melted coating; insert stick into cake ball (no more than halfway through). Return cake pop to baking sheet in refrigerator to set. Repeat with remaining cake balls and sticks.

4. Working with one cake pop at a time, hold stick and dip cake ball into melted coating to cover completely, letting excess coating drip off. Rotate stick gently and/or tap stick on edge of bowl, if necessary, to remove excess coating. Place cake pop in foam block. Immediately attach candy star to top of pop while coating is still wet; hold in place until coating is set.

5. Pipe dots on cake pops with decorator frosting for ornaments.

Makes about 24 pops

Table of Contents

Petite Sweets

Little Chocolate Chip Coffee Cakes

1⅓ cups all-purpose flour
¾ teaspoon baking powder
½ teaspoon salt
¼ teaspoon baking soda
¾ cup packed brown sugar
½ cup (1 stick) butter, softened
¼ cup granulated sugar
1 teaspoon vanilla
2 eggs
½ cup plus 3 tablespoons milk, divided
1½ cups semisweet chocolate chips, divided

1. Preheat oven to 350°F. Generously grease and flour 18 mini (¼-cup) bundt cups. Combine flour, baking powder, salt and baking soda in small bowl.

2. Beat brown sugar, butter, granulated sugar and vanilla in large bowl with electric mixer at medium speed until light and fluffy. Beat in eggs, one at a time, until well blended. Alternately add flour mixture and ½ cup milk, beginning and ending with flour mixture; beat at low speed until blended. Stir in 1 cup chocolate chips.

3. Spoon batter into prepared bundt cups, filling three-fourths full (about 3 tablespoons batter per cup).

4. Bake about 16 minutes or until toothpick inserted into centers comes out clean. Cool cakes in pans 5 minutes. Invert onto wire racks; cool completely.

5. Combine remaining ½ cup chocolate chips and 3 tablespoons milk in small microwavable bowl. Microwave on HIGH 30 seconds; stir. Microwave at 15-second intervals until chocolate is melted and mixture is smooth. Drizzle glaze over cakes. *Makes 18 coffee cakes*

Mini Strawberry Shortcakes

1 quart fresh strawberries, hulled and sliced
½ cup sugar, divided
1 cup all-purpose flour
2 teaspoons baking powder
¼ teaspoon salt
¼ cup (½ stick) cold butter, cut into small pieces
1¼ cups whipping cream, divided

1. Combine strawberries and ¼ cup sugar in medium bowl; set aside.

2. Preheat oven to 425°F. Combine flour, 2 tablespoons sugar, baking powder and salt in large bowl; mix well. Cut in butter with pastry blender or two knives until mixture resembles coarse crumbs. Gradually add ½ cup cream, stirring gently until dough comes together. (Dough will be slightly sticky.) Knead gently 4 to 6 times.

3. Pat dough into 6-inch square on lightly floured surface. Cut dough into 16 (1½-inch) squares with sharp knife. Place 2 inches apart on ungreased baking sheet.

4. Bake about 10 minutes or until golden brown. Remove biscuits to wire rack; cool slightly. Meanwhile, beat remaining ¾ cup cream and 2 tablespoons sugar in medium bowl with electric mixer at high speed until soft peaks form.

5. Split biscuits in half horizontally. Top bottom halves of biscuits with berry mixture, whipped cream and top halves of biscuits.

Makes 16 mini shortcakes

Brownie Ice Cream Treats

½ cup all-purpose flour
½ teaspoon salt
¼ teaspoon baking powder
6 tablespoons (¾ stick) butter
1 cup sugar
½ cup unsweetened Dutch process cocoa powder
2 eggs
½ teaspoon vanilla
8 (2¼-inch) jars with lids
2 cups pistachio or any flavor ice cream, slightly softened
   Hot fudge topping, heated (optional)

1. Preheat oven to 350°F. Spray 9-inch square baking pan with nonstick cooking spray. Combine flour, salt and baking powder in small bowl.

2. Melt butter in medium saucepan over low heat. Stir in sugar until blended. Stir in cocoa until well blended. Stir in eggs, one at a time, then vanilla. Stir in flour mixture until blended. Pour into prepared pan.

3. Bake 20 minutes or until toothpick inserted into center comes out with fudgy crumbs. Cool completely in pan on wire rack.

4. For 2¼-inch-wide jars, cut out 16 brownies using 2-inch round cookie or biscuit cutter. (See Tip.) Remove brownie scraps from pan (any pieces left between round cut-outs); crumble into small pieces. Save remaining brownies for another use.

5. Place one brownie in each of eight ½-cup glass jars. Top with 2 tablespoons ice cream, pressing to form flat layer over brownie. Repeat brownie and ice cream layers.

6. Drizzle with hot fudge topping, if desired, and sprinkle with brownie crumbs. Serve immediately or make ahead through step 5. Cover and freeze until ready to serve.   *Makes 8 servings*

Tip: Measure the diameter of your jar first and cut out your brownies slightly smaller to fit in the jar. If your jar is not tall enough to fit two brownie layers, cut the brownies in half horizontally with a serrated knife.

Mini Peppermint Cheesecakes

2 packages (8 ounces each) cream cheese, softened
1 cup powdered sugar, sifted
1½ teaspoons peppermint extract
1 cup whipping cream
3 to 4 drops red food coloring
25 peppermint candies (about 4 ounces), crushed, divided
1 package mini graham cracker crumb pie crusts (6 crusts)

1. Beat cream cheese, powdered sugar and peppermint extract in medium bowl with electric mixer at medium speed until smooth.

2. Beat cream in small bowl with electric mixer at high speed until stiff peaks form. Stir whipped cream, food coloring and three fourths of crushed peppermints into cream cheese mixture.

3. Divide mixture evenly among pie crusts, mounding mixture in centers. Refrigerate 1 hour or until ready to serve.

4. Just before serving, sprinkle cheesecakes with remaining crushed peppermints.   *Makes 6 cheesecakes*

Tip: Cheesecakes may be made up to 2 days in advance.

Petite Pudding Parfaits

2 ounces bittersweet or semisweet chocolate, chopped
(or about ⅓ cup chips)
2 ounces white chocolate, chopped (or about ⅓ cup chips)
½ cup sugar
2 tablespoons all-purpose flour
1 tablespoon cornstarch
⅛ teaspoon salt
2¼ cups milk
2 egg yolks, beaten
2 teaspoons vanilla
8 (2-ounce) shot glasses
Chocolate curls or grated bittersweet chocolate (optional)

1. Place bittersweet chocolate and white chocolate in separate heatproof bowls; set aside.

2. Combine sugar, flour, cornstarch and salt in small saucepan. Gradually whisk in milk. Cook over medium heat, stirring constantly, until mixture comes to a boil. Boil 2 minutes, stirring constantly.

3. Remove saucepan from heat. Drizzle small amount of hot mixture into beaten egg yolks, stirring constantly; stir egg yolk mixture into saucepan. Cook and stir over low heat until thickened. Remove from heat; stir in vanilla.

4. Spoon half of egg yolk mixture over each chocolate; stir until chocolates are completely melted.

5. Alternate layers of puddings in shot glasses, using about 1 tablespoon pudding for each layer. Cover and refrigerate until chilled. Top with chocolate curls before serving, if desired. *Makes about 8 servings*

Mighty Milkshakes

1 package (about 19 ounces) brownie mix, plus ingredients to prepare mix
1 package (14 to 16 ounces) milk chocolate or peanut butter candy
    coating
½ (16-ounce) container white or vanilla frosting
    Colored drinking straws
    Colored sprinkles

1. Preheat oven to 350°F. Spray 9-inch square baking pan with nonstick cooking spray.

2. Prepare brownie mix according to package directions; pour batter into prepared pan. Bake 35 minutes or until toothpick inserted into center comes out clean. Cool completely in pan on wire rack. Cover and freeze 1 hour or overnight.

3. Run knife around edges of brownies. Place cutting board over baking pan; invert and let stand until brownies release from pan. Trim edges; discard. Cut into 18 rectangles.

4. Place candy coating in medium microwavable bowl; melt according to package directions.

5. Stand brownies up vertically on short side. Spread candy coating on all sides except bottom. Let stand on wire racks 10 minutes or until set.

6. Pipe frosting on top of each brownie to resemble whipped cream. Decorate with straws and sprinkles. *Makes 18 brownies*

Mini Gingerbread Wheat Cakes

¾ cup whole wheat flour
½ cup all-purpose flour
1 tablespoon ground ginger
1½ teaspoons baking powder
1 teaspoon grated orange peel
1 teaspoon ground cinnamon
½ teaspoon salt
¼ teaspoon baking soda
¼ teaspoon ground cloves
¼ teaspoon ground nutmeg
¼ cup (½ stick) butter, softened
¼ cup granulated sugar
¼ cup packed brown sugar
1 egg
½ cup dark molasses
½ cup hot water
Whipped cream

1. Preheat oven to 350°F. Generously grease 6 mini (4-inch) bundt cups; dust lightly with flour.

2. Combine whole wheat flour, all-purpose flour, ginger, baking powder, orange peel, cinnamon, salt, baking soda, cloves and nutmeg in medium bowl.

3. Beat butter, granulated sugar, brown sugar and egg in large bowl with electric mixer at medium speed until light and fluffy. Add molasses; beat until well blended. Add flour mixture alternately with water, beating at low speed just until blended. Divide batter evenly among prepared cups.

4. Bake 20 to 25 minutes or until toothpick inserted near centers comes out clean. Cool in pan 10 minutes. Carefully run knife around inside and outside edge of each cup. Invert on wire rack; cool completely. Serve with whipped cream.   *Makes 6 cakes*

Mini Chocolate Cheesecakes

8 squares (1 ounce each) semisweet baking chocolate, chopped
3 packages (8 ounces each) cream cheese, softened
½ cup sugar
3 eggs
1 teaspoon vanilla

1. Preheat oven to 325°F. Lightly spray 12 standard (2½-inch) muffin cups with nonstick cooking spray.

2. Place chocolate in 1-cup microwavable bowl. Microwave on HIGH 1 to 1½ minutes or until chocolate is melted, stirring after 1 minute. Let cool slightly.

3. Beat cream cheese and sugar in large bowl with electric mixer at medium speed about 2 minutes or until light and fluffy. Add eggs and vanilla; beat about 2 minutes or until well blended. Beat melted chocolate into cream cheese mixture until well blended.

4. Divide mixture evenly among prepared muffin cups. Place muffin pan in larger baking pan; place on oven rack. Pour warm water into larger pan to depth of ½ to 1 inch.

5. Bake 30 minutes or until edges are dry and centers are almost set. Remove muffin pan from water. Cool cheesecakes completely in pan on wire rack.

Makes 12 cheesecakes

Mini Swirl Cheesecakes: Before adding chocolate to cream cheese mixture, place about 2 heaping tablespoons cream cheese mixture in each muffin cup. Add chocolate to remaining cream cheese mixture in bowl; beat until well blended. Spoon chocolate mixture over plain mixture in muffin cups; swirl with knife before baking.

Carrot Cake Minis

1 cup packed light brown sugar
¾ cup plus 2 tablespoons all-purpose flour
1 teaspoon baking soda
½ teaspoon salt
½ teaspoon ground cinnamon
¼ teaspoon ground nutmeg
⅛ teaspoon ground cloves
½ cup canola oil
2 eggs
1½ cups lightly packed grated carrots
½ teaspoon vanilla
Cream Cheese Frosting (recipe follows)
Toasted shredded coconut* (optional)

*To toast coconut, spread evenly in shallow baking pan. Bake in 350°F oven
5 to 7 minutes or until golden brown, stirring occasionally.

1. Preheat oven to 350°F. Line 36 mini (1¾-inch) muffin cups with paper baking cups.

2. Whisk brown sugar, flour, baking soda, salt, cinnamon, nutmeg and cloves in large bowl. Stir in oil until blended. Add eggs, one at a time, stirring until blended after each addition. Stir in carrots and vanilla. Spoon batter evenly into prepared muffin cups.

3. Bake 15 minutes or until toothpick inserted into centers comes out clean. Cool in pans 5 minutes. Remove to wire racks; cool completely.

4. Meanwhile, prepare Cream Cheese Frosting. Frost cupcakes. Sprinkle with coconut, if desired. Store cupcakes covered in refrigerator.

Makes 36 mini cupcakes

Cream Cheese Frosting: Beat 1 package (8 ounces) softened cream cheese and ¼ cup (½ stick) softened butter in medium bowl with electric mixer at medium-high speed until creamy. Beat in ¼ teaspoon salt and ¼ teaspoon vanilla. Gradually beat in 1½ cups sifted powdered sugar until well blended.

Pumpkin Mousse Cups

1¼ cups whipping cream, divided
1 cup canned pumpkin
⅓ cup sugar
½ teaspoon pumpkin pie spice
⅛ teaspoon salt
½ teaspoon vanilla
½ cup crushed gingersnap cookies (about 8 small gingersnaps)

1. Combine ½ cup cream, pumpkin, sugar, pumpkin pie spice and salt in small saucepan; bring to a simmer over medium heat. Reduce heat to low; simmer 15 minutes, stirring occasionally. Stir in vanilla; set aside to cool to room temperature.

2. Beat remaining ¾ cup cream in medium bowl with electric mixer at high speed until soft peaks form. Gently fold 1 cup whipped cream into pumpkin mixture until blended. Refrigerate until ready to serve.

3. Spoon heaping ¼ cup pumpkin mousse into each of eight ½-cup glasses or dessert dishes. Top with dollop of remaining whipped cream; sprinkle with crushed cookies. *Makes 8 servings*

Tip Store leftover canned pumpkin in an airtight container in the refrigerator for up to 1 week or in the freezer for up to 3 months.

Brownie Bites

1 package (about 18 ounces) refrigerated chocolate chip cookie dough
    with fudge filling in squares or rounds (20 count)
¼ cup unsweetened cocoa powder
1½ teaspoons vanilla, divided
1 package (about 16 ounces) refrigerated chocolate chip cookie dough
4 ounces cream cheese, softened
1 cup sifted powdered sugar

1. Spray 30 mini (1¾-inch) muffin cups with nonstick cooking spray. Place chocolate chip cookie dough with fudge filling in large bowl; let stand at room temperature about 15 minutes.

2. Add cocoa and ½ teaspoon vanilla to dough in bowl; beat with electric mixer at medium speed until well blended. Shape dough into 30 balls; press onto bottoms and up sides of prepared muffin cups. Refrigerate 1 hour.

3. Preheat oven to 350°F. Shape chocolate chip cookie dough into 30 balls; place each ball into dough-lined muffin cups. Gently flatten tops if necessary.

4. Bake 14 to 16 minutes. Cool in pans 10 minutes. Remove to wire racks; cool completely.

5. Beat cream cheese and remaining 1 teaspoon vanilla in medium bowl with electric mixer at medium speed, gradually adding powdered sugar until frosting is light and fluffy. Spoon heaping teaspoon frosting onto each cookie.

Makes 30 cookies

Note: Brownie Bites are best served the day they are made. Store leftovers in refrigerator.

Rustic Apple Tartlets

1 tablespoon butter
4 medium Granny Smith, Crispin or other firm-fleshed apples, peeled and cut into ¾-inch chunks (about 4 cups)
6 tablespoons granulated sugar
½ teaspoon ground cinnamon
⅛ teaspoon salt
2 teaspoons cornstarch
2 teaspoons lemon juice
1 refrigerated pie crust (half of 15-ounce package)
1 egg, beaten
1 tablespoon coarse or granulated sugar

1. Melt butter in medium saucepan over medium heat; stir in apples, granulated sugar, cinnamon and salt. Cook 10 minutes or until apples are tender, stirring occasionally. Drain apples in colander set over medium bowl; pour liquid back into saucepan. Cook over medium-high heat until liquid is slightly syrupy and reduced by half. Stir in cornstarch; cook 1 minute.

2. Combine apples, lemon juice and cornstarch mixture in medium bowl; toss to coat. Let apple mixture cool to room temperature.

3. Preheat oven to 425°F. Line large rimmed baking sheet with parchment paper. Unroll dough onto clean work surface; cut out five circles with 4-inch round cookie cutter. Place dough circles on prepared baking sheet.

4. Divide apples evenly among dough circles, piling apples in center of each circle and leaving ½-inch border. Fold edge of dough up over filling, overlapping and pleating dough as necessary. Press dough gently to adhere to filling. Brush dough lightly with beaten egg; sprinkle tartlets with coarse sugar.

5. Bake about 25 minutes or until crusts are golden brown. Cool on wire rack.

Makes 5 tartlets

Mini Black & White Cheesecakes

1 cup chocolate wafer cookie crumbs
12 ounces cream cheese, softened
½ cup sugar
2 teaspoons vanilla
½ cup milk
2 eggs
½ cup semisweet chocolate chips, melted and slightly cooled

1. Preheat oven to 325°F. Line 12 standard (2½-inch) muffin cups with paper baking cups. Spoon rounded tablespoon cookie crumbs into each cup.

2. Beat cream cheese, sugar and vanilla in large bowl with electric mixer at medium speed until light and fluffy. Add milk and eggs; beat until well blended. Transfer half of mixture to medium bowl. Stir in melted chocolate; set aside.

3. Divide remaining plain cream cheese mixture among prepared muffin cups. Bake 10 minutes.

4. Divide chocolate mixture among muffin cups; spread to edges. Bake 15 minutes or until centers are almost set. Cool completely in pan on wire racks. Store in refrigerator. *Makes 12 cheesecakes*

Sweetheart Chocolate Mini Bundt Cakes

1⅔ cups all-purpose flour
½ cup unsweetened cocoa powder
1 teaspoon baking soda
¼ teaspoon salt
1 cup plus 2 tablespoons buttermilk
¾ cup mayonnaise
¾ cup packed brown sugar
1 teaspoon vanilla
1 cup (6 ounces) semisweet chocolate chips, divided
¼ cup whipping cream

1. Preheat oven to 350°F. Spray 6 mini (4-inch) bundt cups with nonstick cooking spray. Combine flour, cocoa, baking soda and salt in medium bowl.

2. Beat buttermilk, mayonnaise, brown sugar and vanilla in large bowl with electric mixer at medium speed until well blended. Gradually add flour mixture; beat 2 minutes or until well blended. Stir in ½ cup chocolate chips. Spoon batter evenly into prepared pans.

3. Bake 22 minutes or until toothpick inserted near centers comes out clean. Cool in pan 15 minutes. Invert onto wire rack; cool completely.

4. Place remaining ½ cup chocolate chips in small bowl. Heat cream in small saucepan over low heat until bubbles form around edge of pan; pour over chips. Let stand 5 minutes; stir until smooth. Cool until slightly thickened; drizzle over cakes.   *Makes 6 cakes*

Cookie Jar Jumble

Little Oatmeal Cookies

¾ cup all-purpose flour
½ teaspoon baking soda
½ teaspoon ground cinnamon
¼ teaspoon salt
½ cup (1 stick) butter, softened
½ cup packed brown sugar
¼ cup granulated sugar
1 egg
1 teaspoon vanilla
1½ cups quick or old-fashioned oats
½ cup raisins

1. Preheat oven to 350°F. Combine flour, baking soda, cinnamon and salt in small bowl.

2. Beat butter, brown sugar and granulated sugar in large bowl with electric mixer at medium speed until creamy. Add egg and vanilla; beat until well blended. Gradually beat in flour mixture at low speed until well blended. Stir in oats and raisins. Drop dough by scant teaspoonfuls 2 inches apart onto ungreased cookie sheets.

3. Bake 7 minutes or just until edges are lightly browned. Cool on cookie sheets 1 minute. Remove to wire racks; cool completely.

Makes about 6 dozen cookies

Quick Walnut Bites

1 package (about 16 ounces) refrigerated sugar cookie dough
¾ cup all-purpose flour
2 tablespoons honey or maple syrup
1 cup chopped walnuts or pecans
¾ cup powdered sugar

1. Let dough stand at room temperature 15 minutes.

2. Beat dough, flour and honey in large bowl with electric mixer at medium speed until well blended. Stir in walnuts. Shape dough into disc; wrap tightly in plastic wrap. Refrigerate at least 2 hours or up to 2 days.

3. Preheat oven to 350°F. Shape dough into ¾-inch balls. Place 1½ inches apart on ungreased cookie sheets.

4. Bake 10 to 12 minutes or until lightly browned. Cool on cookie sheets 2 minutes.

5. Place powdered sugar in shallow dish. Transfer hot cookies to powdered sugar and roll until coated. Remove to wire racks; cool completely. Just before serving, roll cookies in additional powdered sugar.

Makes about 2½ dozen cookies

Tiny Peanut Butter Sandwiches

1¼ cups all-purpose flour
½ teaspoon baking powder
½ teaspoon baking soda
¼ teaspoon salt
½ cup (1 stick) butter, softened
½ cup granulated sugar
½ cup packed brown sugar
½ cup creamy peanut butter
1 egg
1 teaspoon vanilla
1 cup semisweet chocolate chips
½ cup whipping cream

1. Preheat oven to 350°F. Combine flour, baking powder, baking soda and salt in medium bowl.

2. Beat butter, granulated sugar and brown sugar in large bowl with electric mixer at medium speed until light and fluffy. Beat in peanut butter, egg and vanilla until well blended. Gradually beat in flour mixture at low speed until blended.

3. Shape dough by ½ teaspoonfuls into balls; place 1 inch apart on ungreased cookie sheets. Flatten balls slightly in criss-cross pattern with tines of fork.

4. Bake 6 minutes or just until set. Cool on cookie sheets 4 minutes. Remove to wire racks; cool completely.

5. For filling, place chocolate chips in medium bowl. Microwave cream on HIGH 2 minutes or just until simmering; pour over chocolate chips. Let stand 2 minutes; stir until smooth. Let stand 10 minutes or until filling thickens to desired consistency.

6. Spread scant teaspoon filling on flat side of half of cookies; top with remaining cookies. Store in airtight container.

Makes 6 to 7 dozen sandwiches

Mexican Chocolate Macaroons

8 squares (1 ounce each) semisweet chocolate, divided
1¾ cups plus ⅓ cup whole almonds, divided
¾ cup sugar
2 egg whites
1 teaspoon ground cinnamon
1 teaspoon vanilla

1. Preheat oven to 400°F. Grease cookie sheets.

2. Place 5 chocolate squares in food processor; process until coarsely chopped. Add 1¾ cups almonds and sugar; process using on/off pulses until mixture is finely ground. Add egg whites, cinnamon and vanilla; process just until mixture forms moist dough.

3. Shape dough into 1-inch balls. (Dough will be sticky.) Place 2 inches apart on prepared cookie sheets. Press 1 whole almond into center of each dough ball.

4. Bake 8 to 10 minutes or just until set. Cool on cookie sheets 2 minutes. Remove to wire racks; cool completely.

5. Chop remaining 3 chocolate squares; place in small resealable food storage bag. Microwave on HIGH 1 minute; knead bag. Microwave at additional 30-second intervals until chocolate is melted, kneading after each interval. Cut off small corner of bag. Drizzle chocolate over cookies. Let stand until set. *Makes about 3 dozen cookies*

Chocolate-Topped Linzer Cookies

3 cups hazelnuts, toasted, skins removed, divided
1 cup (2 sticks) butter, softened
1 cup powdered sugar, sifted
½ teaspoon grated lemon peel
¼ teaspoon salt
½ egg*
3 cups sifted all-purpose flour
½ cup nougat paste**
½ cup seedless red raspberry jam
6 squares (1 ounce each) semisweet chocolate
2 tablespoons shortening

*To measure ½ egg, lightly beat 1 egg in glass measuring cup; remove half for use in recipe.
**Nougat paste, a mixture of ground hazelnuts, sugar and semisweet chocolate, is available in specialty candy and gourmet food shops. If unavailable, substitute melted semisweet chocolate.*

1. Place 1½ cups hazelnuts in food processor; process until finely ground. (There should be ½ cup ground nuts; if necessary, process additional nuts.) Set aside remaining whole nuts for garnish.

2. Beat butter, powdered sugar, lemon peel and salt in large bowl with electric mixer at medium speed until blended. *Do not overmix.* Add egg; beat until well blended. Stir in ground hazelnuts. Gradually stir in flour. Divide dough into quarters. Wrap each piece in plastic wrap; refrigerate about 2 hours or until firm.

3. Preheat oven to 350°F. Line cookie sheets with parchment paper. Working with one piece at a time, roll out dough to ⅛- to ¹⁄₁₆-inch thickness on lightly floured surface. Cut out circles with 1¼-inch round cookie cutter. Place 1 inch apart on prepared cookie sheets.

4. Bake 7 to 8 minutes or until lightly browned. Cool cookies completely on cookie sheets.

5. Spoon nougat paste into pastry bag fitted with ¼-inch round tip. Pipe about ¼ teaspoon paste onto centers of one third of cookies. Top with plain cookies; press gently.

6. Spoon raspberry jam into pastry bag fitted with ⅓-inch round tip. Pipe about ½ teaspoon jam onto centers of second cookie layers. Top with remaining plain cookies; press gently. Let cookies stand about 1 hour.

7. Melt chocolate and shortening in small heavy saucepan over low heat; stir until smooth. Dip top of each cookie into chocolate mixture just to cover; shake to remove excess chocolate. Place cookies on wire racks. Press whole hazelnut on top of each cookie; let stand until chocolate is set.

Makes about 4 dozen cookies

No-Bake Gingery Date Balls

1½ cups gingersnap crumbs (about 20 gingersnaps)
1 cup finely chopped pecans
1 cup finely chopped dates
½ cup finely chopped candied ginger
¼ teaspoon salt
¾ cup powdered sugar, divided
½ cup light corn syrup

1. Combine gingersnap crumbs, pecans, dates, candied ginger and salt in large bowl; stir until well blended.

2. Add ¼ cup powdered sugar and corn syrup; knead by hand until mixture comes together. Shape into 1-inch balls.

3. Place remaining ½ cup powdered sugar in shallow dish; roll balls in sugar to coat. Place balls in small paper candy cups for serving, if desired.

Makes about 4 dozen cookies

 Tip You can crush the gingersnaps very quickly in a food processor. Or place them a heavy resealable food storage bag, seal the bag and use a rolling pin to crush the cookies into fine crumbs.

One-Bite Pineapple Chewies

½ cup whipping cream
¼ cup sugar
⅛ teaspoon salt
 1 cup finely chopped dried pineapple
½ cup slivered and chopped almonds
¼ cup mini semisweet chocolate chips
¼ cup all-purpose flour

1. Preheat oven to 350°F. Line cookie sheets with parchment paper.

2. Whisk cream, sugar and salt in large bowl until sugar dissolves. Stir in pineapple, almonds and chocolate chips. Stir in flour until blended.

3. Drop dough by rounded teaspoonfuls about 1 inch apart onto prepared cookie sheets.

4. Bake 13 to 15 minutes or until edges are golden brown. Cool on cookie sheets 2 minutes. Remove to wire racks; cool completely.

Makes about 2 dozen cookies

Flourless Peanut Butter Chocolate Chippers

1 cup packed brown sugar
1 cup creamy or chunky peanut butter*
1 egg
  Granulated sugar
½ cup milk chocolate chips

Do not use natural peanut butter.

1. Preheat oven to 350°F.

2. Beat brown sugar, peanut butter and egg in medium bowl with electric mixer at medium speed until well blended.

3. Shape dough into 1½-inch balls. Place 2 inches apart on ungreased cookie sheets. Dip fork into granulated sugar; flatten each ball to ½-inch thickness, crisscrossing with fork. Press 3 to 4 chocolate chips on top of each cookie.

4. Bake 12 minutes or until just set. Cool on cookie sheets 2 minutes. Remove to wire racks; cool completely.   *Makes 1½ dozen cookies*

Festive Fudge Blossoms

¼ cup (½ stick) butter, softened
1 package (about 18 ounces) chocolate fudge cake mix
1 egg, lightly beaten
2 tablespoons water
¾ to 1 cup finely chopped walnuts
48 chocolate star candies

1. Preheat oven to 350°F. Cut butter into cake mix in large bowl with pastry blended or two knives until mixture resembles coarse crumbs. Stir in egg and water until well blended.

2. Shape dough into ½-inch balls. Place walnuts in shallow dish. Roll balls of dough in walnuts; press gently to adhere. Place 2 inches apart on ungreased cookie sheets.

3. Bake 12 minutes or until puffed and nearly set. Place chocolate star in center of each cookie; bake 1 minute. Cool on cookie sheets 2 minutes. Remove to wire racks; cool completely.   *Makes about 4 dozen cookies*

 Tip Purchase nuts in small quantities and store them in a cool, dry and dark place. (Heat, light and moisture encourage rancidity.) They can be stored in an airtight container for up to 4 months in the refrigerator and 8 months in the freezer.

Ginger Molasses Spice Cookies

2 cups all-purpose flour
1½ teaspoons ground ginger
1 teaspoon baking soda
½ teaspoon salt
½ teaspoon ground cinnamon
½ teaspoon ground cloves
1¼ cups sugar, divided
¾ cup (1½ sticks) butter, softened
¼ cup molasses
1 egg

1. Preheat oven to 375°F. Combine flour, ginger, baking soda, salt, cinnamon and cloves in medium bowl.

2. Beat 1 cup sugar and butter in large bowl with electric mixer at medium speed until light and fluffy. Add molasses and egg; beat until well blended. Gradually beat in flour mixture at low speed just until blended.

3. Place remaining ¼ cup sugar in shallow dish. Shape dough by ½ teaspoonfuls into balls; roll in sugar to coat. Place 1 inch apart on ungreased cookie sheets.

4. Bake 7 to 8 minutes or until almost set. Cool on cookie sheets 2 minutes. Remove to wire racks; cool completely. *Makes about 12 dozen cookies*

Mexican Wedding Cookies

1 cup pecan pieces or halves
1 cup (2 sticks) butter, softened
2 cups powdered sugar, divided
2 cups all-purpose flour
2 teaspoons vanilla
⅛ teaspoon salt

1. Place pecans in food processor; process using on/off pulses until pecans are ground but not pasty.

2. Beat butter and ½ cup powdered sugar in large bowl with electric mixer at medium speed until light and fluffy. Gradually add 1 cup flour, vanilla and salt; beat at low speed until well blended. Stir in remaining 1 cup flour and ground pecans. Shape dough into ball; wrap in plastic wrap. Refrigerate 1 hour or until firm.

3. Preheat oven to 350°F. Shape dough into 1-inch balls. Place 1 inch apart on ungreased cookie sheets.

4. Bake 12 to 15 minutes or until golden brown. Cool on cookie sheets 2 minutes.

5. Place 1 cup powdered sugar in 13×9-inch baking dish. Transfer hot cookies to powdered sugar. Roll cookies in powdered sugar, coating well. Let cookies cool in sugar in dish.

6. Sift remaining ½ cup powdered sugar over cookies just before serving. Store tightly covered at room temperature or freeze up to 1 month.

Makes about 4 dozen cookies

Peanut Blossoms

1 package (about 18 ounces) yellow cake mix
1 cup peanut butter
⅓ cup butter, softened
1 egg
¼ cup sugar
50 milk chocolate kiss candies

1. Preheat oven to 350°F. Spray cookie sheets lightly with nonstick cooking spray.

2. Beat cake mix, peanut butter, butter and egg in large bowl with electric mixer at medium speed until well blended.

3. Place sugar in shallow dish. Shape dough into 1-inch balls; roll in sugar to coat. Place 2 inches apart on prepared cookie sheets. Press one candy into center of each ball, flattening dough slightly.

4. Bake 10 minutes or until lightly browned. Cool on cookie sheets 2 minutes. Remove to wire racks; cool completely.

Makes about 4 dozen cookies

 Tip Make sure you allow your cookie sheets to cool to room temperature before using them for additional batches. Placing cookie dough on warm cookie sheets will cause the dough to melt and spread, which will affect the texture and shape of the cookies.

One-Bite Chocolate Chip Cookies

1¼ cups all-purpose flour
½ teaspoon baking soda
¼ teaspoon salt
½ cup (1 stick) butter, softened
½ cup packed brown sugar
¼ cup granulated sugar
1 egg
1 teaspoon vanilla
1¼ cups mini semisweet chocolate chips
Sea salt (optional)

1. Preheat oven to 350°F. Combine flour, baking soda and salt in medium bowl.

2. Beat butter, brown sugar and granulated sugar in large bowl with electric mixer at medium speed until light and fluffy. Beat in egg and vanilla until blended. Add flour mixture; beat at low speed until well blended. Stir in chocolate chips.

3. Drop dough by ½ teaspoonfuls 1 inch apart onto ungreased cookie sheets. Sprinkle very lightly with sea salt, if desired.

4. Bake 6 minutes or just until edges are golden brown. (Centers of cookies will be very light and will not look done.) Cool on cookie sheets 2 minutes. Remove to wire racks; cool completely. *Makes about 14 dozen cookies*

Bite-Size Bars

Peanut Butter Cereal Bars

3 cups mini marshmallows
3 tablespoons butter
½ cup peanut butter
3½ cups crisp rice cereal
1 cup quick oats
⅓ cup mini semisweet chocolate chips

Microwave Directions

1. Spray 13×9-inch baking pan with nonstick cooking spray.

2. Combine marshmallows and butter in large microwavable bowl. Microwave on HIGH 15 seconds; stir. Microwave 1 minute; stir until marshmallows are melted and mixture is smooth.

3. Stir in peanut butter until blended. Add cereal and oats; stir until well coated. Spread in prepared pan. Sprinkle with chocolate chips; lightly press chips into cereal mixture.

4. Cool completely in pan. Cut into bars.   *Makes 40 bars*

Tip To make spreading the cereal mixture easier, lightly spray your spoon with nonstick cooking spray before stirring.

Dark Chocolate Nut Bars

1 package (12 ounces) dark chocolate nuggets with almonds*
1½ cups all-purpose flour
⅓ cup unsweetened Dutch process cocoa powder
1½ teaspoons baking powder
½ teaspoon salt
1 cup (2 sticks) butter, softened
¾ cup packed brown sugar
½ cup granulated sugar
2 eggs
1 teaspoon vanilla
1 cup chopped pecans

Or substitute your favorite candy bars; use enough to make 1½ cups chopped candy.

1. Preheat oven to 350°F. Spray 13×9-inch baking pan with nonstick cooking spray. Chop candy into ¼-inch chunks; refrigerate until ready to use.

2. Combine flour, cocoa, baking powder and salt in small bowl. Beat butter, brown sugar and granulated sugar in large bowl with electric mixer until creamy. Beat in eggs and vanilla until well blended. Stir in flour mixture.

3. Reserve half of chopped candy; stir remaining candy and pecans into dough. Spread dough in prepared pan. Sprinkle with reserved candy.

4. Bake about 25 minutes or until toothpick inserted into center comes out clean. Cut into 1½-inch squares.   *Makes about 4 dozen bars*

Chocolate Dream Bars

1½ cups packed brown sugar, divided
½ cup (1 stick) butter, softened
1 egg yolk
1 cup plus 2 tablespoons all-purpose flour, divided
2 eggs
1 cup (6 ounces) semisweet chocolate chips
½ cup chopped toasted walnuts*

To toast walnuts, spread in single layer on baking sheet. Bake in preheated 350°F oven 5 to 7 minutes or until golden brown, stirring frequently.

1. Preheat oven to 375°F. Spray 13×9-inch baking pan with nonstick cooking spray.

2. Beat ½ cup brown sugar, butter and egg yolk in large bowl with electric mixer at medium speed until light and smooth. Stir in 1 cup flour until well blended. Press dough onto bottom of prepared pan. Bake 12 to 15 minutes or until golden.

3. Meanwhile, beat remaining 1 cup brown sugar, 2 tablespoons flour and whole eggs in same bowl until light and frothy. Spread mixture over partially baked crust.

4. Return to oven; bake about 15 minutes or until topping is set. Immediately sprinkle with chocolate chips. Let stand until chips soften; spread chocolate evenly over bars. Sprinkle with walnuts. Cool completely in pan on wire rack. Cut into bars. *Makes about 4½ dozen bars*

Chocolate Chunk Oat Bars

1 cup all-purpose flour
½ teaspoon baking soda
½ teaspoon salt
1 cup packed brown sugar
½ cup (1 stick) butter, softened
1 egg
1 tablespoon water
1 teaspoon vanilla
1½ cups old-fashioned oats
2 cups semisweet chocolate chunks, divided

1. Preheat oven to 375°F. Lightly spray 9-inch square baking pan with nonstick cooking spray. Combine flour, baking soda and salt in small bowl.

2. Beat brown sugar and butter in large bowl with electric mixer at medium-high speed until creamy. Add egg, water and vanilla; beat until well blended. Stir in flour mixture and oats; mix well. Stir in 1½ cups chocolate chunks.

3. Spread dough evenly in prepared pan; sprinkle with remaining ½ cup chocolate chunks.

4. Bake about 30 minutes or just until center feels firm. Cool completely in pan on wire rack. Cut into bars.   *Makes 3 dozen bars*

Mississippi Mud Bars

1 cup plus 2 tablespoons all-purpose flour
½ teaspoon baking soda
¼ teaspoon salt
¾ cup packed brown sugar
½ cup (1 stick) butter, softened
1 egg
1 teaspoon vanilla
1 cup (6 ounces) semisweet chocolate chips, divided
1 cup (6 ounces) white chocolate chips, divided
½ cup chopped walnuts or pecans

1. Preheat oven to 375°F. Line 9-inch square baking pan with foil; spray foil with nonstick cooking spray. Combine flour, baking soda and salt in small bowl.

2. Beat brown sugar and butter in large bowl with electric mixer at medium speed until well blended. Add egg and vanilla; beat until blended. Add flour mixture; beat until well blended. Stir in ⅔ cup semisweet chips, ⅔ cup white chips and walnuts. Spread dough in prepared pan.

3. Bake 23 to 25 minutes or until center is firm to the touch. *Do not overbake.* Immediately sprinkle with remaining ⅓ cup semisweet chips and ⅓ cup white chips. Let stand until chips soften; spread chocolate evenly over bars. Cool in pan on wire rack until chocolate is set. Cut into triangles.

Makes about 3 dozen triangles

Buttery Oatmeal Turtle Bars

Crust
- 1 cup all-purpose flour
- 1 cup old-fashioned oats
- ¾ cup packed brown sugar
- ½ cup (1 stick) butter, softened
- 1½ cup whole pecans

Topping
- ⅔ cup packed brown sugar
- ½ cup (1 stick) butter
- ½ teaspoon vanilla
- 4 ounces semisweet or milk chocolate, broken into 1-inch chunks

1. Preheat oven to 350°F. For crust, combine flour, oats, ¾ cup brown sugar and ½ cup butter until well blended. Pat firmly into ungreased 13×9-inch baking pan. Sprinkle with pecans.

2. For topping, combine ⅔ cup brown sugar and ½ cup butter in medium heavy saucepan. Cook over medium heat, stirring constantly, until mixture comes to a boil. Boil 1 minute. Remove from heat; stir in vanilla. Pour evenly over pecans and crust.

3. Bake 15 to 18 minutes or until caramel is bubbly.

4. Sprinkle chocolate evenly over caramel layer. Bake 1 minute to melt chocolate. Swirl chocolate for marbled effect. Cool slightly; refrigerate until set. Cut into bars.   *Makes 4 to 5 dozen bars*

Chocolate Chip S'More Bites

1 package (about 16 ounces) refrigerated chocolate chip cookie dough
¾ cup semisweet chocolate chips
¼ cup plus 2 tablespoons whipping cream
½ cup marshmallow creme
½ cup sour cream

1. Preheat oven to 325°F. Spray 13×9-inch baking pan with nonstick cooking spray.

2. Press cookie dough into prepared pan, using damp hands to spread dough into even layer and cover bottom of pan. (Dough will be very thin.) Bake 20 minutes or until light golden brown and just set. Cool in pan on wire rack.

3. Meanwhile, place chocolate chips in medium bowl. Microwave cream on HIGH 1 minute or just until simmering; pour over chocolate chips. Let stand 2 minutes; stir until smooth. Let stand 10 minutes or until mixture thickens.

4. Combine marshmallow creme and sour cream in small bowl until smooth.

5. Cut bars into 1¼-inch squares with sharp knife. For each s'more, spread scant teaspoon chocolate mixture on bottom of one square; spread scant teaspoon marshmallow mixture on bottom of second square. Press together to form s'mores.   *Makes about 4 dozen s'mores*

Chocolate Caramel Bars

2 cups all-purpose flour
1½ cups packed brown sugar, divided
1¼ cups (2½ sticks) butter, softened, divided
1 cup chopped pecans
1 cup (6 ounces) chocolate chips

1. Preheat oven to 350°F.

2. Combine flour, 1 cup brown sugar and ½ cup butter in large bowl until crumbly. Press firmly on bottom of ungreased 13×9-inch pan; sprinkle with pecans.

3. Combine remaining ½ cup brown sugar and ¾ cup butter in medium heavy saucepan. Cook over medium heat, stirring constantly, until mixture comes to a boil. Boil 1 minute, stirring constantly, until blended and smooth. Pour caramel evenly over pecans and crust.

4. Bake 18 to 20 minutes or until caramel layer bubbles evenly all over. Immediately sprinkle with chocolate chips. Let stand 2 minutes or until chips soften; spread chocolate evenly over bars. Let stand until chocolate is set. Cut into bars. *Makes about 4½ dozen bars*

 Tip Adding a slice of bread to a bag of brown sugar that has hardened can help restore its moisture. To soften brown sugar more quickly, place 1 cup sugar in a microwavable bowl, cover with plastic wrap and microwave on HIGH 30 to 45 seconds. Stir and repeat if necessary.

Shortbread Turtle Cookie Bars

1¼ cups (2½ sticks) butter, softened, divided
1 cup all-purpose flour
1 cup old-fashioned oats
1¼ cups packed brown sugar, divided
1 teaspoon ground cinnamon
¼ teaspoon salt
1½ cups chopped pecans
6 squares (1 ounce each) bittersweet or semisweet chocolate, finely chopped
4 squares (1 ounce each) white chocolate, finely chopped

1. Preheat oven to 350°F.

2. Beat ½ cup butter in large bowl with electric mixer at medium speed 2 minutes or until light and fluffy. Add flour, oats, ¾ cup brown sugar, cinnamon and salt; beat at low speed until coarse crumbs form. Press firmly on bottom of ungreased 13×9-inch baking pan.

3. Combine remaining ¾ cup butter and ¾ cup brown sugar in medium heavy saucepan. Cook over medium heat, stirring constantly, until mixture comes to a boil. Boil 1 minute without stirring. Remove from heat; stir in pecans. Pour evenly over crust.

4. Bake 18 to 22 minutes or until caramel begins to bubble. Immediately sprinkle with bittersweet and white chocolates; swirl (do not spread) with knife after 45 seconds to 1 minute or when slightly softened. Cool completely in pan on wire rack. Cut into bars.   *Makes about 4½ dozen bars*

Dandy Candy

Crème Brûlée Fudge

2½ cups granulated sugar
½ cup (1 stick) butter, cubed
1 can (5 ounces) evaporated milk
½ package (6 ounces) white chocolate chips
1 jar (7 ounces) marshmallow creme
1½ teaspoons vanilla
3 tablespoons turbinado sugar

1. Line 13×9-inch baking pan with foil, extending foil over edges of pan. Spray foil with nonstick cooking spray.

2. Combine granulated sugar, butter and evaporated milk in large heavy saucepan. Bring to a boil over medium heat, stirring constantly. Reduce heat to medium-low; boil, stirring constantly, until candy thermometer reads 234°F (soft-ball stage).

3. Remove from heat. Add white chocolate chips, marshmallow creme and vanilla, stirring constantly until chocolate melts and mixture becomes satiny. Immediately pour into prepared pan (do not scrape side of saucepan) and spread evenly.

4. Preheat broiler. Sprinkle top of fudge with turbinado sugar. Broil 1 to 2 minutes or until turbinado sugar melts and top browns (watch carefully). Let stand at room temperature until cool. Refrigerate until firm. Use foil to lift fudge out of pan. Remove foil and cut into squares. *Makes 2½ pounds fudge*

Note: Turbinado sugar is made by evaporating the juice from sugar cane. The result is coarse crystals with a golden color. It is natural and unrefined, and its flavor has a hint of molasses.

Tropical Cookie Balls

1 cup crushed coconut bar cookies (about 8 cookies)
1 bag (6 ounces) tropical medley dried fruit, finely minced*
¼ teaspoon salt
1½ cups finely chopped pecans, divided
1½ cups sweetened shredded coconut, divided
½ teaspoon ground cinnamon
⅓ cup light corn syrup
2 tablespoons honey
1 teaspoon rum extract

Or substitute 1 cup minced dried fruits, such as mango, pineapple, golden or dark raisins and papaya.

1. Combine cookie crumbs, dried fruit and salt in large bowl; mix well. Add 1 cup pecans, ½ cup coconut and cinnamon; mix well.

2. Stir in corn syrup, honey and rum extract; knead by hand until mixture comes together. Shape into 1-inch balls.

3. Combine remaining ½ cup pecans and 1 cup coconut in shallow dish; roll balls in mixture to coat.   *Makes about 3 dozen treats*

 Tip To make cookie crumbs, place cookies in a food processor; process until finely ground. Or place cookies in a resealable food storage bag and use a rolling pin to crush the cookies into fine crumbs.

Mint Chocolate Fudge Squares

6 squares (1 ounce each) white chocolate, chopped
1 container (16 ounces) vanilla frosting, divided
4 to 6 drops peppermint extract, divided
3 drops red or green food coloring
8 squares (1 ounce each) semisweet chocolate, divided
½ teaspoon vegetable oil

1. Spray 8-inch square baking pan with nonstick cooking spray. Line bottom and sides of pan with parchment paper or waxed paper.

2. Combine white chocolate and half of frosting in medium microwavable bowl. Microwave on HIGH 1½ minutes, stirring every 30 seconds, until melted and smooth. Add 2 to 3 drops peppermint extract and food coloring; mix well. Spread evenly in prepared pan. Refrigerate 15 minutes or until set.

3. Coarsely chop 1 square semisweet chocolate; set aside for garnish. Coarsely chop remaining semisweet chocolate; place in medium microwavable bowl. Add remaining frosting; microwave on HIGH 1½ to 2 minutes, stirring every 30 seconds, until melted and smooth. Add remaining 2 to 3 drops peppermint extract; mix well. Stir 1 to 2 minutes, allowing mixture to cool. Carefully pour mixture over white chocolate layer; spread evenly. Cover and refrigerate 30 minutes or until set.

4. Lift fudge from pan using parchment paper; carefully invert onto cutting board and remove paper. Place reserved semisweet chocolate and oil in small microwavable bowl. Microwave on HIGH 1 minute or until melted, stirring every 30 seconds. Drizzle melted chocolate over fudge.

5. Cover and refrigerate 20 to 30 minutes or until firm. Cut into 1-inch squares. Store in airtight container in refrigerator.   *Makes 64 squares*

Toffee Chocolate Crispies

1 cup slivered almonds
1 cup crisp rice cereal
½ cup milk chocolate toffee bits
1 cup milk or semisweet chocolate chips
1 teaspoon shortening

1. Line large baking sheet with foil. Place almonds in medium nonstick skillet; toast over medium heat, stirring frequently, 7 to 8 minutes or until lightly browned. Place almonds in large bowl; stir in cereal and toffee bits.

2. Place chocolate chips and shortening in medium microwavable bowl. Microwave on HIGH 30 seconds; stir. Microwave at additional 10-second intervals; stir until melted and smooth. Pour chocolate mixture over almond mixture; stir until evenly coated.

3. Drop mixture by rounded tablespoonfuls onto prepared baking sheet. Refrigerate 30 minutes or until cool and firm. Serve immediately or store between layers of waxed paper in airtight container in refrigerator up to 1 week. *Makes about 27 candies*

White Chocolate Triangles

1 cup white chocolate chips
½ cup sweetened condensed milk
½ cup chopped pecans, toasted*
½ (9-ounce) package chocolate wafers, crushed

To toast pecans, spread in single layer on baking sheet. Bake in preheated 350°F oven 8 to 10 minutes or until golden brown, stirring frequently.

1. Spray 8-inch square baking pan with nonstick cooking spray.

2. Combine white chocolate chips and condensed milk in medium saucepan; cook and stir over low heat until chocolate is melted. Stir in pecans and crushed wafers.

3. Spread mixture in prepared pan; let stand until set. Cut into triangles. Serve chilled or at room temperature. Store tightly covered in refrigerator.

Makes 6 dozen triangles

Malted Milk Balls

2½ cups small malted milk balls (½-inch diameter), coarsely crushed
1¾ cups chocolate graham cracker crumbs (9 to 11 crackers)
  3 tablespoons unsweetened cocoa powder, divided
  ¼ teaspoon salt
  1 cup mini marshmallows
  ½ cup light corn syrup
  1 tablespoon honey
  1 teaspoon rum extract
  ½ cup powdered sugar

1. Combine malted milk balls, graham cracker crumbs, 2 tablespoons cocoa and salt in large bowl; mix well. Chop marshmallows with remaining 1 tablespoon cocoa. Add to malted milk ball mixture; stir until blended.

2. Add corn syrup, honey and rum extract; knead by hand until mixture comes together. Shape into 1-inch balls.

3. Spread powdered sugar in shallow dish; roll balls in sugar to coat.

Makes about 4 dozen treats

Tip: To make graham cracker crumbs, place crackers in food processor; process until finely ground. Or place crackers in resealable food storage bag and use a rolling pin to crush the crackers into fine crumbs. Malted milk balls can also be crushed in a resealable food storage bag.

Variation: Substitute 1 teaspoon vanilla for the rum extract. Roll balls in unsweetened cocoa powder.

After-Dinner Mocha Truffle Cups

36 Chocolate Cups (recipe follows) or purchased chocolate liqueur cups
1 cup whipping cream
2 eggs
1 cup (6 ounces) semisweet chocolate chips
2 tablespoons prepared espresso, cooled
1 tablespoon coffee-flavored liqueur
1 teaspoon unflavored gelatin

1. Prepare Chocolate Cups; set aside.

2. Place large bowl and beaters from electric mixer in freezer until cold. Beat cream in chilled bowl with electric mixer at high speed until soft peaks form. Refrigerate until ready to use.

3. Beat eggs in medium bowl with electric mixer at high speed about 5 minutes or until thick and lemon colored.

4. Heat chocolate chips in top of double boiler over hot, not boiling, water, stirring until melted. Remove from heat. Stir ¼ cup melted chocolate into beaten eggs. Stir egg mixture into remaining melted chocolate; cook over medium heat 1 minute, stirring constantly. Remove from heat.

5. Combine espresso and liqueur in small bowl; sprinkle with gelatin. Let stand 1 minute to soften. Gradually add gelatin mixture, a few drops at a time, to chocolate mixture, whisking until smooth.

6. Gently fold half of chocolate mixture into chilled whipped cream. Add to remaining chocolate, gently folding until combined. Spoon chocolate mixture into Chocolate Cups with small spoon. Refrigerate at least 3 hours or until firm.

Makes 3 dozen candy cups

Chocolate Cups

1 package (12 ounces) semisweet chocolate chips
1 tablespoon shortening
36 small foil candy cups

1. Heat chocolate chips and shortening in top of double boiler over hot, not boiling, water, stirring until melted. Remove from heat.

2. Spoon about ½ tablespoon melted chocolate into each candy cup. Brush chocolate up side of cups with small, clean craft paintbrush, coating foil completely. Carefully wipe off any chocolate that may have run over top of foil cup using tip of finger. Place cups on baking sheet; let stand in cool place until firm. (Do not refrigerate.)

3. To remove foil from cups, cut slits in bottom of foil cups and peel foil up from bottom. (Do not peel down from top edge.) *Makes 3 dozen cups*

Chocolate-Cherry Balls

1 cup chocolate graham cracker crumbs (6 to 7 crackers)
1 cup mini chocolate chips
¾ cup butter cookie crumbs (8 to 10 cookies)
⅛ teaspoon salt
½ cup prepared chocolate fudge frosting
¼ cup dark corn syrup
1 teaspoon vanilla
   About 72 dried cherries
½ cup powdered sugar

1. Combine graham cracker crumbs, chocolate chips, cookie crumbs and salt in large bowl; mix well.

2. Add frosting, corn syrup and vanilla; knead by hand until mixture comes together. Shape into 1-inch balls.

3. Press 2 dried cherries into center of each ball; reshape mixture around cherries to cover.

4. Spread powdered sugar in shallow dish; roll balls in sugar to coat.

Makes about 3 dozen treats

Variation: Roll balls in unsweetened cocoa powder.

 Tip To make graham cracker and cookie crumbs, place crackers and cookies in a food processor; process until finely ground. Or place the crackers and cookies in resealable food storage bag and use a rolling pin to crush them into fine crumbs.

Scrumptious Truffles

Truffles

10 ounces semisweet chocolate, chopped
2 tablespoons butter, cut into pieces
2 to 3 tablespoons brandy (optional)
¾ cup whipping cream

Coatings

½ cup unsweetened cocoa
¼ cup pistachio nuts or hazelnuts, finely chopped
14 ounces semisweet, milk or white chocolate

1. Place chopped chocolate, butter and brandy, if desired, in large bowl. Bring cream to a boil in medium saucepan over medium heat. Pour over chocolate mixture; stir until smooth. Refrigerate 6 hours or overnight.

2. Place cocoa in shallow dish. Shape chocolate mixture into small balls; roll balls in cocoa to coat.

3. For pistachio truffles, omit cocoa and roll balls in chopped pistachios. Wrap in plastic wrap and chill up to 10 days.

4. For chocolate truffles, omit cocoa and freeze truffles 1 hour. Melt desired flavor of chocolate. Dip balls in melted chocolate; place on parchment-lined baking sheet and refrigerate until ready to serve.

Makes about 1 pound truffles

Tropical Sugarplums

½ cup white chocolate chips
¼ cup light corn syrup
½ cup chopped dates
¼ cup chopped maraschino cherries, well drained
1 teaspoon vanilla
¼ teaspoon rum extract
1¼ cups gingersnap cookie crumbs
1 cup flaked coconut

1. Combine white chocolate chips and corn syrup in medium saucepan. Cook and stir over low heat until chocolate is melted and mixture is smooth. Remove from heat.

2. Stir in dates, cherries, vanilla and rum extract until well blended. Add gingersnap crumbs; stir until well blended. (Mixture will be stiff.)

3. Place coconut in shallow dish. Shape gingersnap mixture into ¾-inch balls; roll in coconut to coat. Place in mini paper candy cups, if desired. Serve immediately or let stand overnight to allow flavors to blend.

Makes about 2 dozen candies

Peanut Butter Truffles

2 cups (11½ ounces) milk chocolate chips
½ cup whipping cream
2 tablespoons butter
½ cup creamy peanut butter
¾ cup finely chopped peanuts

1. Combine chocolate chips, cream and butter in medium heavy saucepan; melt over low heat, stirring occasionally. Add peanut butter; stir until blended. Pour into pie pan. Refrigerate about 1 hour or until mixture is fudgy but soft, stirring occasionally.

2. Shape mixture by tablespoonfuls into 1¼-inch balls; place on waxed paper.

3. Place peanuts in shallow dish. Roll balls in peanuts; place in paper candy cups. (If peanuts won't stick because truffle has set, roll truffle between palms until outside is soft.) Store truffles in refrigerator 2 to 3 days.

Makes about 3 dozen truffles

Mocha Fudge

1¾ cups sugar
¾ cup whipping cream
1 tablespoon instant coffee granules
1 tablespoon light corn syrup
1 cup (6 ounces) milk chocolate chips
1 cup (half of 7-ounce jar) marshmallow creme
½ cup chopped nuts
1 teaspoon vanilla

1. Butter 8-inch square pan. Lightly butter side of medium heavy saucepan.

2. Combine sugar, cream, coffee granules and corn syrup in prepared saucepan. Cook over medium heat, stirring constantly, until sugar is dissolved and mixture comes to a boil. Wash down side of saucepan with pastry brush frequently dipped in hot water to remove sugar crystals. Boil 5 minutes.

3. Meanwhile, combine chocolate chips, marshmallow creme, nuts and vanilla in heatproof bowl.

4. Pour sugar mixture over chocolate mixture; stir until chocolate is melted. Spread evenly in prepared pan. Score fudge into squares with knife. Refrigerate until firm.

5. Cut into squares. Store covered in refrigerator.

Makes about 1¾ pounds fudge

Coconut Bonbons

2 cups powdered sugar
1 cup flaked coconut
3 tablespoons evaporated milk
2 tablespoons butter, softened
1 teaspoon vanilla
1 cup (6 ounces) semisweet chocolate chips
1 tablespoon shortening
　Toasted coconut (optional)
　Melted white chocolate (optional)

1. Line baking sheet with waxed paper.

2. Combine powdered sugar, coconut, evaporated milk, butter and vanilla in medium bowl; mix well. Shape mixture into 1-inch balls; place on prepared baking sheet. Refrigerate until firm.

3. Combine chocolate chips and shortening in small microwavable bowl. Microwave on HIGH 1 minute; stir. Microwave at 30-second intervals, stirring after each interval, until chocolate is melted and mixture is smooth.

4. Dip bonbons in melted chocolate using toothpick or wooden skewer. Remove excess chocolate by scraping bottom of bonbon across rim of bowl; return to prepared baking sheet.

5. Sprinkle some bonbons with toasted coconut, if desired. Refrigerate all bonbons until firm. Drizzle plain bonbons with melted white chocolate, if desired. Store in refrigerator.　　*Makes about 3 dozen bonbons*

Gift Idea: Place the bonbons in petit fours or paper candy cups. Arrange crinkled paper gift basket filler in the bottom of a tin or gift box and nestle the candies in the filler. Or for party favors or small gifts, place 3 or 4 bonbons in a cellophane bag and tie it with colored curling ribbon.

Chunky Peanut Butter Fudge

1 cup powdered sugar
1 cup sweetened condensed milk
1 cup creamy peanut butter
2 tablespoons butter
½ teaspoon vanilla
1 cup chopped peanuts, divided

Microwave Directions

1. Line 8-inch square baking pan with parchment paper, extending 1 inch over edges of pan. Grease paper.

2. Combine powdered sugar, condensed milk, peanut butter, butter and vanilla in medium microwavable bowl. Microwave on HIGH 1 minute; stir. Microwave 1 minute; stir until butter is melted. Stir in ¾ cup peanuts.

3. Spread mixture evenly in prepared pan. Sprinkle with remaining ¼ cup peanuts. Cover and refrigerate 2 hours or until firm.

4. Remove fudge with parchment paper from pan. Place on cutting board; peel off paper. Cut into ½-inch squares. Store covered in refrigerator.

Makes about 5 dozen squares

Classic Rum Balls

2 cups vanilla cookie crumbs (about 60 vanilla wafers)
2 cups powdered sugar, divided
1 cup finely chopped walnuts or pecans
2 tablespoons unsweetened cocoa powder
¼ teaspoon salt
½ cup light corn syrup
1 tablespoon honey
2 teaspoons rum extract
½ teaspoon vanilla

1. Combine cookie crumbs, 1 cup powdered sugar, walnuts, cocoa and salt in large bowl; mix well.

2. Add corn syrup, honey, rum extract and vanilla; knead by hand until mixture comes together. Shape into 1-inch balls.

3. Place remaining 1 cup powdered sugar in shallow dish; roll balls in sugar to coat.   *Makes 4 to 5 dozen treats*

Two-Bite Treats

Brownie Buttons

½ cup (1 stick) butter
2 squares (1 ounce each) unsweetened chocolate
1 cup sugar
2 eggs, at room temperature
½ cup all-purpose flour
¼ teaspoon salt
1 teaspoon vanilla
½ cup semisweet chocolate chips
¼ cup whipping cream
   Small chocolate nonpareil candies

1. Preheat oven to 325°F. Spray 8-inch square baking pan with nonstick cooking spray.

2. Melt butter and unsweetened chocolate in small heavy saucepan over low heat. Remove from heat; gradually stir in sugar. Beat in eggs, one at a time, until blended. Stir in flour and salt. Stir in vanilla. Spread batter evenly in prepared pan.

3. Bake 25 to 28 minutes or until firm in center and toothpick inserted into center comes out with fudgy crumbs. Cool completely in pan on wire rack; refrigerate until cold.

4. Use 1¼-inch round cookie or biscuit cutter to cut out circles from brownies. Place brownies on wire rack set over waxed paper.

5. Place chocolate chips in small bowl. Microwave cream on HIGH 1 minute or just until simmering; pour over chocolate chips. Let stand 1 minute; stir until smooth. Let stand several minutes to thicken slightly; pour mixture over tops of brownies. Place candy in center of each brownie.

Makes about 2 dozen brownies

Jelly Doughnut Bites

½ cup plus 3 tablespoons warm (95° to 105°F) milk, divided
1¼ teaspoons active dry yeast
⅓ cup granulated sugar
1 tablespoon butter, softened
2½ cups all-purpose flour
1 egg
½ teaspoon salt
½ cup raspberry jam
Powdered sugar

1. Stir 3 tablespoons warm milk and yeast in large bowl until blended; let stand 5 minutes. Add granulated sugar, butter and remaining ½ cup milk; mix well. Add flour, egg and salt; beat with dough hook of electric mixer at low speed until dough starts to climb up dough hook. If dough is too sticky, add additional flour, 1 tablespoon at a time. Or knead dough on lightly floured surface until smooth and elastic.

2. Transfer dough to greased medium bowl; turn dough over to grease top. Cover and let stand in warm place 1 hour.

3. Spray 48 mini (1¾-inch) muffin cups with nonstick cooking spray. Punch down dough. Shape pieces of dough into 1-inch balls; place in prepared muffin cups. Cover and let rise 1 hour.

4. Preheat oven to 375°F. Bake 10 to 12 minutes or until light golden brown. Remove to wire racks; cool completely.

5. Place jam in pastry bag fitted with small round tip. Insert tip into side of each doughnut; squeeze about 1 teaspoon jam into center. Sprinkle filled doughnuts with powdered sugar. *Makes 4 dozen doughnut bites*

Tip These doughnuts are best eaten the same day they are made. They can be served warm or at room temperature. If desired, microwave on HIGH 10 seconds just before serving.

Tiramisu Shots

¾ cup milk
4 ounces cream cheese, softened
1 package (1¼ ounces) dark chocolate hot cocoa mix
1 cup coffee ice cream
2 tablespoons cold strong coffee
1 tablespoon amaretto liqueur (optional)
1 teaspoon powdered sugar
12 chocolate cordial cups (optional)
  Whipped cream (optional)
  Chocolate-covered espresso or coffee beans (optional)

1. Combine milk, cream cheese and hot cocoa mix in blender; blend until smooth. Add ice cream, coffee, amaretto, if desired, and powdered sugar; blend until smooth.

2. Pour into chocolate cordial cups or shot glasses. Garnish with whipped cream and chocolate-covered espresso beans. *Makes 12 servings*

No-Bake Gingersnap Balls

20 gingersnap cookies (about 5 ounces)
3 tablespoons dark corn syrup
2 tablespoons creamy peanut butter
⅓ cup powdered sugar

1. Place cookies in large resealable food storage bag; crush finely with rolling pin or meat mallet.

2. Combine corn syrup and peanut butter in medium bowl. Add crushed gingersnaps; mix well. (Mixture should hold together without being sticky. If mixture is too dry, stir in additional 1 tablespoon corn syrup.)

3. Place powdered sugar in shallow dish. Shape gingersnap mixture into 24 (1-inch) balls; roll in powdered sugar to coat.

Makes 2 dozen cookies

Tip: Some gingersnaps are crisper than others, so you might need to add an additional 1 to 2 tablespoons corn syrup to the crumb mixture in order to hold it together.

Oriental Chews

1 package (6 ounces) chow mein noodles
1 cup flaked coconut
1 cup (6 ounces) semisweet chocolate chips
1 cup (6 ounces) butterscotch-flavored chips
1 package (3 ounces) slivered almonds

1. Preheat oven to 350°F. Place noodles and coconut on cookie sheet in single layer. Bake 10 minutes or until crisp.

2. Melt chocolate and butterscotch chips in top of double boiler over hot, not boiling, water. Remove from heat; stir in almonds, noodles and coconut.

3. Drop mixture by teaspoonfuls onto waxed paper. Let stand until set.

Makes about 5 dozen chews

No-Bake Cherry Crisps

1 cup powdered sugar
1 cup peanut butter
¼ cup (½ stick) butter, softened
1⅓ cups crisp rice cereal
½ cup maraschino cherries, drained, dried and chopped
¼ cup plus 2 tablespoons mini semisweet chocolate chips
¼ cup chopped pecans
1 to 2 cups flaked coconut

1. Beat powdered sugar, peanut butter and butter in large bowl with electric mixer at medium speed until well blended. Stir in cereal, cherries, chocolate chips and pecans.

2. Place coconut in shallow dish. Shape teaspoonfuls of mixture into 1-inch balls; roll balls in coconut to coat.

3. Place on cookie sheets and refrigerate 1 hour. Store cookies between sheets of waxed paper in airtight container in refrigerator.

Makes about 3 dozen treats

Mocha Cookie Balls

1¾ cups chocolate graham cracker crumbs (9 to 11 crackers)
1½ cups (8 ounces) chocolate-covered coffee beans, coarsely chopped
1 cup finely chopped walnuts
1 teaspoon instant espresso powder (optional)
¼ teaspoon salt
¾ cup dark corn syrup
1 teaspoon vanilla
½ cup powdered sugar

1. Combine graham cracker crumbs, coffee beans, walnuts, espresso powder, if desired, and salt in large bowl; mix well.

2. Stir in corn syrup and vanilla; knead by hand until mixture comes together. Shape into 1-inch balls.

3. Place powdered sugar in shallow dish; roll balls in sugar to coat.

Makes about 4 dozen cookies

Tip: To make cookie crumbs, place cookies in a food processor; process until finely ground. Or place the cookies in a resealable food storage bag and use a rolling pin to crush the cookies into fine crumbs.

Variation: Roll the balls in unsweetened cocoa powder. Or omit the chocolate-covered coffee beans and instant coffee powder; substitute 1½ cups coarsely chopped bite-size chocolate-covered toffee pieces.

Mini Fruitcake Cupcakes

¾ cup all-purpose flour
½ teaspoon *each* baking powder, ground ginger and ground cinnamon
¼ teaspoon *each* salt and ground allspice
1½ cups dried fruit (raisins, cherries, cranberries, dates, chopped figs
    or apricots)
½ cup Port wine or orange juice
⅓ cup granulated sugar
5 tablespoons butter
¼ cup brown sugar
2 eggs
2 tablespoons orange juice
1 teaspoon grated orange peel
½ cup chopped pecans, toasted
1 cup powdered sugar
3 tablespoons lemon juice

1. Preheat oven to 350°F. Line 28 mini (1¾-inch) muffin cups with paper baking cups or spray with nonstick cooking spray. Whisk flour, baking powder, ginger, cinnamon, salt and allspice in medium bowl.

2. Combine dried fruit and Port wine in medium microwavable bowl. Cover and microwave on HIGH 1 minute. Stir; microwave 1 minute. Let stand 15 minutes or until cool.

3. Beat granulated sugar, butter and brown sugar in large bowl with electric mixer at medium speed until combined. Add eggs, one at a time, beating until blended after each addition. Add orange juice and orange peel; beat until blended.

4. Gradually add flour mixture to butter mixture, beating until blended after each addition. Stir in fruit mixture and pecans. Spoon batter evenly into prepared muffin cups.

5. Bake 15 minutes or until toothpick inserted into centers comes out clean. Cool in pans 5 minutes. Remove to wire racks.

6. Meanwhile, combine powdered sugar and lemon juice in small bowl. Brush glaze over cupcakes while still warm; cool completely on wire racks.

Makes 28 mini cupcakes

Tip: If you don't have mini muffin pans, arrange mini foil baking cups on ungreased cookie sheets. Fill and bake as directed, being careful to spoon batter into the center of the cups so they do not tip over.

Tiny Hot Fudge Sundae Cups

1 package (about 16 ounces) refrigerated sugar cookie dough
⅓ cup unsweetened cocoa powder
5 to 7 cups vanilla ice cream
　Hot fudge ice cream topping, colored sprinkles and whipped cream
9 maraschino cherries, cut into quarters

1. Let dough stand at room temperature 15 minutes. Spray outsides
of 36 mini (1¾-inch) muffin cups with nonstick cooking spray.

2. Preheat oven to 350°F. Beat dough and cocoa in large bowl with
electric mixer at medium speed until well blended. Divide dough into
36 equal pieces; shape each piece over outside of prepared muffin cup.

3. Bake 10 to 12 minutes or until set. Cool on pans 10 minutes. Remove
to wire racks; cool completely.

4. Fill each cooled cookie cup evenly with ice cream. Drizzle with hot fudge
sauce; top with sprinkles. Garnish each sundae cup with whipped cream
and cherry quarter. Serve immediately.　　　*Makes 3 dozen sundae cups*

 Tip Ice cream is often too hard to scoop when it's right out of
the freezer. To soften it quickly, place a 1-quart container
of hard-packed ice cream in the microwave and heat at
MEDIUM (50%) about 20 seconds or just until softened.

Little Christmas Puddings

1 can (14 ounces) sweetened condensed milk
1 ounce semisweet chocolate
2 teaspoons vanilla
2¼ cups chocolate sandwich cookie crumbs
⅓ cup white chocolate chips
  Green sprinkles
  Small red candies

1. Combine sweetened condensed milk and semisweet chocolate in medium saucepan; cook and stir over low heat until chocolate is melted and mixture is smooth. Remove from heat; stir in vanilla.

2. Stir in cookie crumbs until well blended. Cover and refrigerate 1 hour.

3. Line baking sheet with waxed paper. Shape heaping teaspoonfuls of chocolate mixture into 1-inch balls. Place on prepared baking sheet. Refrigerate until firm.

4. Place balls in 1¾-inch paper or foil baking cups on baking sheets. Place white chocolate chips in small microwavable bowl. Microwave on MEDIUM (50%) 1 minute or until melted, stirring after 30 seconds. Spoon melted white chocolate over tops of balls; top with sprinkles and red candies. Let stand until set. Store covered in refrigerator.   *Makes about 3½ dozen treats*

Tiny Toffee Pops

1 pint (2 cups) chocolate ice cream
1½ cups chocolate-covered toffee chips
½ cup finely chopped blanched almonds
½ cup finely chopped milk chocolate
14 lollipop sticks

1. Line baking sheet with plastic wrap. Scoop rounded tablespoonfuls of ice cream onto baking sheet. Freeze 2 hours or until firm.

2. Combine toffee chips, almonds and chocolate in shallow dish; mix well. Gently roll ice cream balls in mixture, turning to coat and press mixture evenly into ice cream. Return to baking sheet.*

3. Insert sticks into ice cream balls. Freeze 2 hours or until firm.

Makes 14 pops

*If ice cream melts on baking sheet, place baking sheet and ice cream in freezer 30 minutes before continuing. If ice cream is too hard, let stand 1 to 2 minutes before rolling in toffee mixture.

Tip You can find lollipop sticks in the baking section of craft stores. These stores also carry a wide variety of decorative paper baking cups; use the small cups to serve the pops. They make an fun and attractive presentation and also keep the pops from melting on a serving tray.

Coffee Brownie Bites

1 package (about 21 ounces) fudge brownie mix
3 eggs
½ cup vegetable oil
2 teaspoons instant coffee granules
2 teaspoons coffee liqueur (optional)
    Powdered sugar (optional)

1. Preheat oven 325°F. Lightly spray 60 mini (1¾-inch) muffin cups with nonstick cooking spray.

2. Combine brownie mix, eggs, oil, coffee granules and coffee liqueur, if desired, in medium bowl; stir until well blended. Spoon 1 tablespoon batter into each prepared muffin cup.

3. Bake 13 minutes or until toothpick inserted into centers comes out almost clean. Remove to wire racks; cool completely.

4. Sprinkle with powdered sugar, if desired. Store in airtight container.

Makes 5 dozen brownies

Nutty Cookie Balls

1½ cups butter cookie crumbs (about 22 butter cookies)
1 cup chopped honey-roasted peanuts
½ cup chopped golden raisins*
½ cup shredded sweetened coconut
5 tablespoons light corn syrup
2 tablespoons honey
2 tablespoons smooth or crunchy peanut butter
⅓ cup unsweetened cocoa powder

Spray knife with nonstick cooking spray to prevent sticking.

1. Combine cookie crumbs, peanuts, raisins and coconut in large bowl; mix well.

2. Add corn syrup, honey and peanut butter; knead by hand until mixture comes together. Shape mixture into 1-inch balls.

3. Place cocoa in shallow dish; roll balls in cocoa to coat.

Makes 2 to 3 dozen cookies

Variation: If desired, roll balls in finely ground peanuts, powdered sugar, shredded coconut or melted chocolate.

 Tip To make cookie crumbs, place cookies in a food processor; process until finely ground. Or place the cookies in a resealable food storage bag and use a rolling pin to crush them into fine crumbs.

METRIC CONVERSION CHART

VOLUME MEASUREMENTS (dry)

$1/8$ teaspoon = 0.5 mL
$1/4$ teaspoon = 1 mL
$1/2$ teaspoon = 2 mL
$3/4$ teaspoon = 4 mL
1 teaspoon = 5 mL
1 tablespoon = 15 mL
2 tablespoons = 30 mL
$1/4$ cup = 60 mL
$1/3$ cup = 75 mL
$1/2$ cup = 125 mL
$2/3$ cup = 150 mL
$3/4$ cup = 175 mL
1 cup = 250 mL
2 cups = 1 pint = 500 mL
3 cups = 750 mL
4 cups = 1 quart = 1 L

VOLUME MEASUREMENTS (fluid)

1 fluid ounce (2 tablespoons) = 30 mL
4 fluid ounces ($1/2$ cup) = 125 mL
8 fluid ounces (1 cup) = 250 mL
12 fluid ounces ($1 1/2$ cups) = 375 mL
16 fluid ounces (2 cups) = 500 mL

WEIGHTS (mass)

$1/2$ ounce = 15 g
1 ounce = 30 g
3 ounces = 90 g
4 ounces = 120 g
8 ounces = 225 g
10 ounces = 285 g
12 ounces = 360 g
16 ounces = 1 pound = 450 g

DIMENSIONS

$1/16$ inch = 2 mm
$1/8$ inch = 3 mm
$1/4$ inch = 6 mm
$1/2$ inch = 1.5 cm
$3/4$ inch = 2 cm
1 inch = 2.5 cm

OVEN TEMPERATURES

250°F = 120°C
275°F = 140°C
300°F = 150°C
325°F = 160°C
350°F = 180°C
375°F = 190°C
400°F = 200°C
425°F = 220°C
450°F = 230°C

BAKING PAN SIZES

Utensil	Size in Inches/Quarts	Metric Volume	Size in Centimeters
Baking or Cake Pan (square or rectangular)	$8\times8\times2$	2 L	$20\times20\times5$
	$9\times9\times2$	2.5 L	$23\times23\times5$
	$12\times8\times2$	3 L	$30\times20\times5$
	$13\times9\times2$	3.5 L	$33\times23\times5$
Loaf Pan	$8\times4\times3$	1.5 L	$20\times10\times7$
	$9\times5\times3$	2 L	$23\times13\times7$
Round Layer Cake Pan	$8\times1 1/2$	1.2 L	20×4
	$9\times1 1/2$	1.5 L	23×4
Pie Plate	$8\times1 1/4$	750 mL	20×3
	$9\times1 1/4$	1 L	23×3
Baking Dish or Casserole	1 quart	1 L	—
	$1 1/2$ quart	1.5 L	—
	2 quart	2 L	—